GRATEFULLY BROKEN

TONEKIA WILLIAMS

Published by Simene' Walden

P.O. BOX 442, MOUNT RAINIER, MD 20712

© 2021 Tonekia Williams

ISBN: 979-8-9851678-1-8

To book the author, please contact her directly.

If you are interested in discounts for bulk purchases or to use any part of this book, please email: williamstee86@gmail.com

Cover Design by Iskanderua

Editing by Simene' Walden | J. Flowers Olnowich

All scripture quotations, unless otherwise noted, are taken from the King James Bible.

Scripture quotations, noted KJV, are taken from the King James Bible. Copyright ©1979, 1980, 1982, 1984 by Thomas Nelson, Inc. Used by permission.

Acknowledgements

All my life I've said to myself, "My family should have a TV show". I honestly thought no one had been through more pain and trauma than us. It's so amazing that no matter what myself or my family has been through, we never lost our faith in God. You want to know what's funny? This book is only half of my testimony.

Mommy you mean the world to me! My drive, my heart, my sense of humor, I get it all from you. I can't wait to spoil you really big! Aunt Jazz, your sacrifices made me who I am today. I love you like a fat kid loves licking the cake mix bowl. Last, but most importantly, Gramma. Your death took the biggest toll on myself and the family. I still don't know how we all remained sane. Well partially sane. What keeps us going is the idea of making you proud. No one went harder for us than Clatis "Our Angel" Williams. We love you old lady. This book is dedicated to you!

During the pandemic, I was alone for 90% of the time. God literally guided me with this whole book project and sent some angels my way to assist me! Simene' Walden, wow. I can't wait until the whole world finally knows who you are. What a blessing you are to me, this project, and so many others. When I think about God's goodness, I get choked up.

I would also like to honor my spiritual parents Omar and Makita Morton. There has been lots of warfare concerning this book, however, I am thankful for you. You showed me how to war in the spirit realm and come against it all!

Contents

Gramma's House

And this is the plan: At the right time he will bring everything together under the authority of Christ-- everything in heaven and on earth accordingly.

-Ephesians 1:10

⋙

Hello 911!" I shouted in astonishment. I found my grandmother on the floor and she's not breathing.

"Can you feel a heartbeat?" said the calm operator on the other end of the line.

"Listen, get someone here now!" I shouted.

After those words, everything went black. What felt like an outer body experience lasted for a few moments. When I regained consciousness, unbeknownst to me, my hands were pumping on grandmother's chest while performing CPR. The pumps became frantic while trying to revive someone so precious to me. To no avail, she continued to lay on the cold bathroom floor lifeless.

Boom Boom Boom!!

I ran to my neighbor's house and banged on their door like the NYPD.

1

Gratefully Broken

"Help me please!!!"

"My grandmother is on the floor. Please come."

A Spanish woman with wet hair came to the door with Tequila smelling breath.

"Ok mami, go back and call the cops. I'm coming."

I blankly ran back. Grandma was still there, in the same position: pants down, eyes closed, and laying on the bathroom floor.

When I left home that morning, I knew something was wrong. On my train ride to Manhattan, a feeling of heaviness took over me. When the crowded, hot, and delayed A-train reached Fulton Street, I ran off. Once I got to my desk, before taking off my coat, I dialed my grandmother's number.

"Hello," a low sleepy voice whispered.

Trying to sound as cheerful as I could, I replied, "Hi old lady, what cha doing?"

She laughed and said, "Oh nothing."

Still, the familiar voice I clung to wasn't so familiar. I knew something was wrong. We chatted for a few minutes, cracked a few jokes, and then I proceeded to ask her about our dinner menu for the evening. My grandmother was my personal chef and she took pride in feeding her family. My love for cooking comes from my Gramma. Cooking is a love language I received from the love of my life. 5pm couldn't come fast enough that day. My mind was very clouded and my work phone would not stop ringing. I kept having the urge to leave early or to yell at the top of my lungs, but I did neither. I knew the first of the month was coming and I had bills to pay. The struggle was real! While walking out the building to head home, I made a mad dash to the train station, bypassing the usual people that congregated outside to say their farewells.

While walking, I dialed my mom.

When she answered, I yelled, "Maaama!!"

"What silly?" she replied while chuckling.

"Nothing much," I replied. "You spoke to your grams today?"

"Nope," she said, "I called her earlier and went by the house, but she didn't answer."

I was about to climb up the fire escape and knock on the window. She waited for me to reply but I just shook my head. One thing about my mama: she's very serious about her family. Rain, sleet, or snow, she would come to check on her loved ones.

"Oh lord ma, she was probably asleep. I'll call you when I get there."

Her last statement was, "I'm worried."

While walking up the stairs to gramma's house, my legs felt like they weighed a ton. I kept hearing my mother's voice in my head,

"I'm worried." Things went blank again and the anxiety I kept avoiding was slipping back up on me. Little did I know, once I stepped inside, my life would never be the same.

Before I knew it, my house was flooded with EMT's, family, paramedics, nosey neighbors, and cops. I regained consciousness once I spotted an EMT worker mis-manhandling my grandmother's body. At that very moment, every ounce of my Brooklyn attitude came out. I nudged the man who was 3 times my size and asked him why he was being so rough? He turned around, but he paid no attention to me.

Next thing I knew, all the workers began to walk out one by one.

Oh yes, they're leaving, I said excitedly.

I tapped a friendly looking sister with short hair and asked, "She's ok, right?"

I guess I was in denial.

"No, she's gone sis," she replied nonchalantly, then walked away.

I responded by throwing my only means of communication to the ground so hard it shattered the screen. Selfishly, I wished I could have left the house too.

"Is Gramma gone?" I thought to myself. "Nah, I need to go somewhere and wake up."

My grandmother laid on her black leather couch, wrapped in her patchwork blanket for over two hours before the coroner showed up. She looked so peaceful. We all gathered around her and gazed in astonishment. Our whole world, our protector, our personal chef, our investor, our pastor, our comedian, our fashion consultant, and our therapist was lying right in front of us lifeless.

I was the spitting image of my grandmother. Wherever she went, her little Tee Tee (which is my nickname) was right behind. My grandmother was smart, determined, and admirable. I strived to be just like her. Clatis was such an integral person who did things from the kindness of her heart. She was never moved by the opinions of others. She was the orchestrator and finisher. Dainty yet feisty described her so well. She was all of 5 ft. 2 inches and was equipped with a bang. Don't let the height fool you; she packed such a powerful punch.

Clearly, I remember my mom dating a 6'4 300 lb. man at one time. I'm sure I wasn't more than six years old. My mom was head over heels about him, but he was mentally and physically abusive. In the streets of Brooklyn, he was a vicious hitman. However, he had a soft spot for my beautiful mother until she disagreed with one of his commands. At that point he would cut off his lavish spending and become hands on with her.

One day my mom came home disoriented from a scuffle with Darren. The next time my grandmother saw Mr. Darren, she gave him a few choice words. Her face barely reached his chest, yet

5

Clatis poked him in the highest area her hands could reach. Very calmly yet authoritative, she stated "If you touch my goddamned daughter again, you're going down." She kindly ended her sentence with one of her favorite lines: "Try me." She then walked off as if she had a gang of mobsters behind her watching her back. That woman was nothing to play with.

Clatis learned her survival tactics by being the black sheep of her family. Her reality turned sour quickly. In the 1950's, she made her way from North Carolina to New York City. She left everything she knew behind, including her family and child, and she vowed to get situated and return with more to offer. She made the mistake of falling for a smooth talker, who promised to marry her after she got pregnant. I'm pretty sure her family didn't understand her reasoning and frowned upon her for leaving her baby boy. My grandmother wanted to go up north to get a job that would secure herself a better lifestyle. Working on someone's farm or field wasn't going to cut it.

Even when your decisions make no sense to others, cast your cares on the Lord for only he can judge us. She wanted a new beginning; to escape her harsh reality.

Clatis entered the world with a partial disadvantage. She was named after my great grandfather's ex-girlfriend. I can imagine that being a hard pill to swallow for my great grandmother. My grandmother always felt she was treated differently due to that matter. When Clatis made her way up north, she had no idea she would eventually meet someone who was going to sweep her off her feet. The same feet she'd been kicked off so many times. Franklin D. Williams was just another ladies man, yet Clatis was vulnerable and fell again.

I recall hearing many stories of my grandmother approaching his "lady friends" but you ain't hear it from me. Based on the things my grandmother went through, I could probably write an entire book on her life. What I found hard to believe was the fact that she didn't drink, smoke, or go to the club.

She worked her 9-5 government job and returning home to her family was her joy. After she made a finger licking meal for her loved ones, she would then proceed to the club couch to watch her favorite shows: Cops, Unsolved Mysteries, and Seven Heaven. You couldn't pay her to change the channel when Seven Heaven came on. I am literally rolling my eyes.

From the union of Clatis and Franklin, five children were born and each of them were very peculiar. Their two boys died by the tender age of twenty-eight and the three beautiful girls all struggled with this thing called life. Oh, and my uncle who stayed behind down south, also died before the age of 30. Talk about tragedy.

From the outside looking in, you could bet your last dollar that my family had it all together. Each of the five children attended Catholic School and lived comfortably in a two-parent home. My grandfather owned two successful businesses at that time. Little did the spectators know, each child rebelled due to the dysfunction behind closed doors. Franklin battled with alcoholism and mental health issues which became the culprit for physical abuse towards my grandmother.

My grandfather's side of the family was known for heavy drinking, bipolar disorders, as well as other mental health issues. After many years of suffering from verbal and physical abuse, my grandmother decided to hit the road with her five children in tow. Her youngest at the time was six years old, but that didn't allow that to stop her. Music artist R Kelly said it best, "When a woman's fed up, there is nothing you can do about it"!

Franklin aka Frankie passed away on March 9, 1996. It was the same day that the rapper Biggie Smalls died. It was such a sad day for Bed Stuy Brooklyn as they had lost two generals. Biggie Smalls lost his life due to a public rap rivalry while Franklin Williams lost his life due to police brutality.

Officers were called to a dispute that was taking place with my grandfather and his much younger girlfriend Shelly. Shelly was at least twenty years my grandfather's junior. After a couple years of dating my grandfather, she picked up a nasty habit of smoking crack. From this dysfunctional unit, two children were fathered after my grandmother filed for divorce. When the police were called to the quiet brown stone-filled block, no one would ever imagine the horrible ending.

My grandfather tried to reason with the police officers, but his cries were unheard. He made the life-shattering mistake of going to retrieve a lotto ticket out of his dirty work pants pocket that he had left on the bathroom floor. When he returned to the house, he noticed another man was there visiting Shelly. There was a tussle, my grandfather was kicked down a flight of stairs, resulting in a trip to the police station. Franklin walked in, yet he never walked back out.

My grandfather was released but he was transported on a stretcher. His destination was to the morgue. Only God knows what happened behind those walls. It baffles me how an elderly man who walked with a limp was such a threat. A charismatic jokester summed up my grandfather's personality. He was born on July 3rd and his personality represented the firecrackers that came on the very next day of his birth. Well known and loyal is what his friends described him as. He didn't deserve to die in such a manner.

He was robbed of his life, his future, and chance of being a part of his children and grandchildren's lives. When my aunt went to view her dad's body, she noticed there were dried tears on his face. I'm sure his life flashed before his eyes and he couldn't believe what was happening.

When my grandmother attempted to go forth and build a case, she was threatened. "We know where you live. You could be next," said an unknown voice, while calling from multiple blocked numbers. Needless to say, my grandmother never thought about suing again. She wanted to protect her children and grandchildren.

My family had it pretty rough. As I piece together details about our history, I often wondered if other families were able to relate with the things we went through. Our dysfunction had become so normal to us.

Clatis Williams taught me about Jesus from a very tender age. I can remember her taking me to church as a toddler. By the age of seven, I was on the usher board and the choir. My beloved grandmother also had me in summer camps at church. Clatis was very serious about her family having a relationship with Christ. We were all rooted in a great foundation no matter how things turned out. Each one of her children and grandchildren were loved, spoiled, and given the best she could provide. Losing the foundation of our family shifted our values. Gramma's death brought isolation, conflict, and misery to the Williams family. Life without her was dark.

A few months before she died, I had just been newly hired for my first city job, making a pretty decent salary at my age. God was giving me a way to provide for myself. One thing about our Heavenly Father is He will never leave nor sake us. My Aunt Sheryl was my grandmother's oldest daughter who had worked for the city for over twenty years. We had our differences, yet I was thankful for her helping me secure my new job.

I was always able to count on my aunt for advice, motivation, and knowledge. If she was still alive today, her ambition and faith would have probably elevated her to the top of the corporate scale. The enemy has a way of attacking the minds of the strongest family members. Sheryl was our rock. She was the member of our family whom we depended on for strength and guidance. Pray for your family members, brothers, and sisters; they are constantly under attack. My aunt Sherly was one of the few family members who died a horrible death. I'll share details later in the story. I hope you're ready.

Right before my grandmother died, life was going well for me. I was attending college, working a career-based job, and I thought I had found the love of my life. Kenny was 6'3, stocky and chocolatey. He was just my type!

We both attended the same college, so I figured God had sent me my husband early in the game. I was nothing less than elated and I'll never forget how we met. College days were so much fun. Truth be told, I was only attending college to make my grandmother proud, and oh to show off my fancy outfits and boots. By the way, guys, I absolutely love boots!

Sadly, I had no intention of taking college seriously. I was there to be seen. Kenny and his friend noticed me one early morning while I was headed to school. At first, I wasn't interested. After a few days of hot pursuit, he started to wear me down. After a week,

I was bringing him hot breakfast to school. Shaking my head! The rest was pretty much history.

After about a year of intense, inseparable dating with Kenny, gramma was called home. Kenny and I were left to hold the apartment down which was not easy. We had all created so many memories together. This was a hard transition for both of us as we had never been on our own before, especially in a home my grandmother was just found dead in. I appreciated him so much more that he stayed around to help me cope with losing her. Not sure what went wrong, but after a while there became an invisible line that separated us.

Communicating was hard and I started to view Kenny in a weird light. Shortly after doing some snooping, I received some information that I really didn't want to find. Instead of calling it quits, I started to retaliate. The attention of other people fed a false need in me. In a shameful way, it made me feel empowered. Long story short, Kenny started cheating and so did I.

My family members referred to my grandmother's apartment as "mommies house," which was understandable. I constantly battled with myself as I knew my grandmother's death was still fresh. However, after months everyone had keys to come and go as they pleased, yet the bills were being paid by myself and Kenny every single month.

For months, we complied, but after a while we became agitated about being overruled in mommy's house. This home was built on love. However, as adults, we required privacy and at least four drama-free nights per week. We had no privacy and no comfort, which also created a strain between us. We understood that we had only three options: move into a new apartment, change the locks, or just deal with it. We chose to deal with it for as long as we could.

The stress level was high with the family and it was becoming unbearable with Kenny. When the realization fell upon me, it hit me like a Mike Tyson punch. I was losing my best friend and soulmate. Guilt started to take over me. Many thoughts started to attack my mind at once:

1. I felt as though I should have been more attentive to my grandmother in her last months of living. Instead, I was consumed in a relationship.

2. Why was I letting my family dictate my relationship?

3. Lastly and drum roll please. Was this Karma for the way I met Kenny?

My mind was a complete wreck. My grandmother was a champ. One year prior to her death, she had beaten breast cancer. Ironically a heart attack one year later claimed her life. Talk about the devil being busy. Talk about generational curses! Shesh. I battled with guilt for years. I was overwhelmed but I knew God was in control and it was His will, not mine. Everything that had taken place was already written. Negative thoughts about my grandmother attempted to consume me for years. Anxiety, depression, shame, and bitterness did its best to bind me up.

It was not until I had suffered for ten years in the same cycles that I finally broke free. The grip of the enemy was no comparison to the love of God for me. I forgave myself and asked God to forgive me for anything I had done knowingly or unknowingly that was not of him. Psalm 55:22 (KJV) declares, "Cast your burdens on the lord, and he shall sustain you. Give your burdens to God."

Tonekia Williams

"Punk Rock"

For you formed my inward parts; you knitted me together in my mother's womb. I praise you, for I am fearfully and wonderfully made. Wonderful are your works; my soul knows it very well. Psalms 139:13-14

It wasn't rare to wake-up in the middle of the night to banging noises at the door when I was a young girl. I would wipe my eyes, make sure I was hearing right, and head to see what the commotion was. Before I could get to the front door, my aunt Jasmine would block me. "Don't open that door, that's your mother trying to get in. I could hear my mother yelling, "Open the door for mommy." I knew my aunt was protecting me and my grandmother, yet I wanted my mom inside where it was safe. I also knew once my mother came in, she would raise hell, fight my aunt, and keep the whole building up all night. At one point my mother would go through these episodes at least three times a week. The people in my apartment building didn't like my mother. On countless occasions, we were close to being evicted. It was so embarrassing. My family and I always felt like we were being watched and scrutinized. When I would walk home from school, I made sure to check my surroundings. My mom had a bad habit of being outside misbehaving or fighting with the neighborhood drunks. One day, after leaving school, I walked to my corner bodega. The Reggaeton music was booming. When you grew up in Bushwick, you learned to appreciate a good Reggaeton track. Ayeeeee!

I walked in the store and noticed there were racks all over the place. Lays and Dorito chips were scattered on the ground. I locked eyes with my friend Mexico, my nickname for the Mexican store clerk. He started shaking his head. "Mami," he said to me with his thick accent, to get my attention. "Tell Ju Mami she can't come here no mas." He was speaking Spanglish. That's half English and half Spanish.

"You see," he said, pointing to the mess on the floor. "No mas mami."

I turned around and took a long walk of shame home. Why couldn't my mom be normal? My mother was the only daughter out of three who birthed a child. Many people had a hard time understanding this reality. How could Tonya the "wild child" be blessed with a baby girl? My two aunts, Jasmine and Sheryl were way more balanced. Still, they didn't have children of their own. I believe it's safe to say I was chosen.

I always knew God had a divine plan for my life; still that didn't stop me from going against a commandment. I was guilty. I hated my mom for hating herself. There were good role models in my life. A plethora of aunts, cousins, uncles, and people who cared about my well-being. But still, the broken little girl that dwelled in me wanted love and attention from my mommy, Tonya. Mothers are our first teachers and role models. Children who don't have healthy bonds with their mothers are susceptible to detachment issues as they grow up. Attachment issues are treatable, yet, if you don't take care of them, they could cause a huge burden in your teenage and adult life. Trust me. Shoutout to my Theories of Counseling Professor Keshia.

Just a word of advice to parents. Do your best to raise children who won't need to heal from your parenting. No man, job, or addiction should come before your role as a parent. Children need love at home, so they won't seek substitutions. Let's break that cycle and continue striving for better than what we may have received.

As a child, I wondered if my mother loved me. Now I know the answer without a doubt. If God forgave my mother, why wouldn't I? While talking to my mom one day, we had a heart-to-heart talk.

I asked her what tragedies she had faced in her life. She answered, "Where do I start?" She recalled decades ago when her and her best friend Audrey had crossed Malcolm X Blvd in Brooklyn. Both were ten years old at the time. They were racing to the store to grab some penny candies. Yes, guys there was once penny candies. She continues, "The light suddenly changed but Audrey wasn't fast enough. Her little legs weren't equipped for the huge

2-way street." When my mother turned around to check on her friend, little Audrey was laid out on the floor. My mother paused for a second and took a big gulp, as if she swallowed her words. In a soft whisper she said, "Tee, the impact of the bus knocked Audrey's head off her shoulders. At her funeral, the head of a doll baby was stitched on Audrey's tiny body."

A month later, the same scenario took place. My mom was crossing the street with her friend Daniel. A drunk driver was speeding and didn't notice the two small children. Tonya walked away without a scratch. Daniel wasn't so lucky. The collision claimed his life. In my 35 years of living, I had never had a heart-to-heart conversation with my mom like that, but I can guarantee that these two traumatic occurrences had a major impact on my mother's mind. To think, at ten years old, her brain was only around 45% developed.

To the person who is reading this book: Your mom may have also been introduced to trauma at a young age. God doesn't make any mistakes. My mom suffered early in life with many traumatic situations that resulted in her becoming a rebellious teen who dropped out of school at fourteen. As an adult, my mother was involved in many mental and physical abusive relationships. I can also guarantee that those early crisis moments shaped who she became as an adult. Drugs and alcohol became an escape for my mother's troubled mind. According to nctsn.org, 59% of young people have suffered from post-traumatic stress disorder and as a consequence they develop substance abuse problems.

Mothers!! We forgive you. Now forgive yourself!

We never expected you to be perfect or raise perfect children. Motherhood doesn't come with a manual. Continue to try your best and we promise to love you unconditionally.

Maybe our mothers and grandmothers suffered as children as well. If they never healed from their hurt, how could they operate in wholeness with us? Whatever the circumstances maybe, it stops now.

Let us pray. "Father God, I thank you for restoring my relationship with my mother. I lift my mother and myself up to you in prayer. Please heal us of past trauma and give us a new beginning. I repent for my sins and my mother's sins. I ask for a renewal in our mind and body. I plead 2 Corinthians 5:7 over our lives. Thank you, Father, for hearing my prayer. In Jesus mighty name I pray. Amen."

If I had a title for my mom's life, it would be called "Cocoon." I've always admired how beautiful my mother is inside and out. No matter the shade of lipstick she wore, it still couldn't hide the pain behind her beautiful smile. At the age of fifty-six, my mother is still very unique and stylish. She has been wearing the brightest shade of red lipstick since I've been in pampers. Tonya simply created style!

Attending the infamous Boys and Girls High School in BedStuy, she received the nickname "Punk Rock" from all the cool kids. My mom and her big sister Sheryl went to all the neighborhood thrift stores and salvation army "boutiques" to recreate their own looks. They started their own fashion movement. In the 70s, they were remixing 1960's Lucy outfits and swagging it out. For those who have no idea who Lucy was, she was the main character from the "I LOVE LUCY" show. I hope I'm not telling my age.

That show was a classic. Go check it out.

"Yo, Tee Tee, those chicks couldn't stand me, I gave them a fever!!"

My mom would randomly say that to me while belting out a loud chuckle.

"I had finger waves and I would come through with my pointy lucy shoes. No one was up on that."

I absolutely love hearing my mom's old stories especially when her eyes would light up. I knew from the childlike excitement in her tone there was something left behind, not just the pointy shoes. My mommy wasn't able to complete the metamorphosis process. Where was the butterfly? Why was she stuck in the process?

My mom had such drive, such talent, and such creativity. In her early twenties she recorded songs and even had a private meeting with a huge record label. Her voice was pretty bomb; however, my mother's downfall was being loyal to the wrong people.

The record company wanted her as a solo act. Nonetheless, "Ms. Loyalty" wanted to bring her friend along. A few years later, that same male friend kidnapped her and held my mom hostage. For years, he had a major crush on my mother, but Tonya didn't think it was a good idea to take the friendship to a deeper level. She enjoyed creating music with him with no strings attached. Moral of that story: pray for discernment. Sometimes we carry the wrong people with us and they become our downfalls.

I remember one song my mom would sing when I was no older than five give or take. "Hanging out on the street corner, life just passing by," she would sing in her sweet voice that reminded me of Anita Baker mixed with Fantasia. This was my mother's way of bringing awareness to a life of unproductivity. How ironic? With her beauty, style, and grace, she could have taken this world by storm.

Tonya was innovative, before her time, and a legend in her own way. When mommy got drunk, she always recited the same story to me. I can remember sitting on the bed while she got dressed to go outside. She slipped on a sequin gold shirt and blue ripped jeans. She always put on her best when she was "going to the store." She would say, "Mommy be right back I'm going to the store to get some cigarettes." I wanted to believe her, even as a young child I knew lies when I heard them. She grabbed her Black leather Michael Jackson inspired tassel jacket, put two coats of her devil red lipstick on, and headed for the door. I almost ran behind her but that never worked. My little legs weren't fast enough. Instead, I went upstairs to hang with my Aunty Jazz. She always had time for me, no matter what. She was something like my best friend. When mommy didn't come home from the night before, she would take me to high school with her in the mornings. To this day, she will not let me forget that. Love you Aunty! Without you, I'm not sure where I would be.

Uncle Carl was my aunt's longtime boyfriend. They were basically joined at the hip. He was about 6'4 350 lbs. and always wore the flyest Karl Kani outfits. I hope Karl cut him a check because he used to represent Karl in all flavors. He kept me fly as well, wearing the latest of everything: bomber jackets, two-finger rings; all the good stuff. Whenever he shopped, he always bought three pairs of everything. One for me, one for my aunty, and one for himself. Don't ask me where he got the money from. I just recall me sporting the best of everything.

When mommy came back from the store, it was always the next day. She would still be dressed like she had just left the runway. The only difference was she would be disoriented and wrecking cigarettes. Her first stop would always be the bathroom.

"Tee Tee," she yelled, "Come help your mama."

When I got there she would be on the floor in her usual spot.

"Take off mommy shoes and pull these pants off for me."

This became our weekly bonding time. I was taking care of mommy. Her pants were always wet, yet she would make a joke out of it. That was her silly personality.

"Mommy couldn't hold it any longer."

I guess on the walk home she just let loose. I quickly helped her and then ran to wash my hands. That part always grossed me out, but I didn't care as long as she was home safely. Anxiety levels would always rise when she left the house. When she returned, I could finally breathe again. I got tired of running back and forth to the window looking for her to come down the block. After I cleaned her up, I would help her change and then wait for her to get up and come to bed. She was too heavy to move, so every 30 minutes I would go check on her laying on the bathroom floor. When she finally decided to get up, she would tell me the same story every time.

"You know you should have two brothers, right? Grandma made me have two abortions. I was young but I wanted my babies. She beat me when I was pregnant with you too, but only on my legs though. I told her, 'You can beat me all you want ma, I'm keeping this baby.'"

That's exactly what she did! I wonder what life would be like if my mother had two other children. I also wonder what affect those two forced abortions had on her mentally and spiritually. My mom was twenty-two when I was born. To be honest, I can't imagine a 22-year-old Tonya with three children. My mother had been through hell and back. For as long as I can remember, she always battled with abusive men, keeping jobs, and addictions. The incredible part is you never caught her in a bad mood.

Talking about someone who cracks jokes, laughs all day, and dances to every sound of music. My mother will literally talk to anyone, help old people cross the street, and share her last with you. Thinking of this just makes me smile so hard. Shout-out to someone who wouldn't let their circumstances break them. I love you Mommy!

I admire my mom's grind and determination. She's very passionate about the things that truly matters to her. Her family was always on the top of the list; right after her man at the current time. Sorry, but men were always my mother's first drug of choice. Tonya tended to put the men in her life before herself. I once battled wit that trait. Thank God for deliverance. I remember when the world was being affected by Hurricane Sandy in 2012. Homes, businesses, even the train stations were flooded. People were encouraged to stay home. It was raining cats and dogs, outside and it looked like someone was throwing buckets of water off roofs. At that time, my mother lived about twenty minutes away from me, on Sumpter Avenue in

Brooklyn. She was not able to get on a bus, train, or cab to get to me. So, she walked. Again, I love you Mommy! It's so amazing to see how over the last few years our relationship has blossomed. When I decided to forgive her for the things she couldn't control, God started working wonders in our lives. Proverbs 17:9 states, "Love prospers when a fault is forgiven." We can't live a holy life if we're holding grudges. God won't honor that. John 4:8 states, "He that loveth not knoweth not God; for God is love." God is love so if we're involved in anything that doesn't reflect the Lord, we're not living right. Harboring and living with hatred, hurt, and unforgiveness in my heart was being defiant to the word of my God. Let's forgive our parents.

Let's remember, like us, they are human beings. No one is perfect. One thing about that enemy is he doesn't like (U.N.I.T.Y.) John 10:10:29 exclaims, "The thief comes only to steal and kill and destroy."

Matter of fact, go call or text your parents now.

I'll wait. Let me know how that goes for you. Praying it goes well.

Daddy Issues

Above all, love each other deeply, because love covers a multitude of sins.

1 Peter 4:8

I'm down the block sweets; be there in 10 mins."

"Ok daddy," I said excitedly.

After doing a happy jiggle, I ran to the bathroom to finish curling my Kool-Aid red hair. Talk about an experiment gone wrong.

"That's what you get for being fast and grown," said my aunt Sheryl every time she looked at my bright hair.

As if that made things any better. I was 14 and in an experimental stage; I did learn my l lesson from the hard way. Before I could even finish my last curl, the loud doorbell started to ring. I ran to the intercom and yelled, "Who is it?"

A deep voice answered back, "It's your father, open the door."

I jumped up and down like a giddy schoolgirl. About ten years had passed since the last time I had seen him. My father went to jail when I was only three years old. I was able to visit him a handful of times, even though I hated the process. It seemed as if you were signing your life away in order to see your loved ones. As a young child, I found it strange being patted down and going through metal detectors to enter the building. The scariest part about the visitation was not knowing who I was in the public visitation room with you. I would play a guessing game every time someone walked out for their visit. I called it, "I wonder what they're in for." It helped me past time from awkward pauses with my father. Sadly, everyone had a story. I can bet my last dollar, most of the inmates were locked up due to childhood trauma that was never fixed. I often wondered what my father lacked that caused him to continuously go to jail. The visits were about two hours long. It mainly consisted of me sitting around trying to figure out if I had his eyes, smile, or personality. I was clueless. I barely knew the man who controlled so many of my emotions. Our relationship was summed up of dispersed fifteen-minute phone conversations, holiday packages, and pictures in the mail for eleven years of my life. In my mind, I knew things would get better; until then I would take what I could get. The rides back home felt like eternity. I had a chance to settle my thoughts. One thought that never failed me was "Why was everyone else so lucky to have their father in their lives?"

I ran down the stairs as if my life depended on it. We met on the second-floor landing and hugged each other intensely. This hug felt so warm and safe. It was exactly what I was missing for a decade.

"Wow baby girl, look at you." he said in amazement.

All I could do was smile and thank God that this moment had finally come. My

protector is home. "I can finally live a normal life," I thought to myself while I clung on to him for dear life. Little did I know, he was only staying for 30 minutes.

His flight was leaving early in the morning to go to Colorado to start his new life.

We sat and chatted for a little while and reminisced about a few things. It was pretty awkward though. I felt as if I was talking to a stranger. I didn't know much about my father; his favorite meal, music, or past time. I had no clue about any of that. I didn't even know if he preferred Martin or Fresh Prince of Bell-Aire.

However, Martin is the greatest, hands down. Thirty minutes surely wasn't enough time to get the answers to my questions, but I understood he had to go away to make a new life for himself.

New York wasn't the right place for him to live. He grew up in the crack era, where there were two options: you were smoking crack or selling it. He was a mover and a shaker. A flashy fly boy who always flaunted his cash. To his advantage, ladies loved that type of stuff—well, the ones he was attracted to. Caramel skin, curly hair, and a smile that was worth millions.

He was the man the ladies wanted and the cool dude other men wanted to be. Growing up, he lived a sheltered life. My strong grandparents didn't play with their kids. On weekends the whole family took trips to live a suburban lifestyle. They wanted the very best of everything for their children. After a while, my father stopped taking those long trips. He thought it was a better idea to stay behind in Brooklyn with his friends.

My grandmother who was a teacher, made a deal with him.

"You bring me a diploma from high school and you can have more freedom."

That's exactly what he did. I can recall my mom's story of how they met. It was spring of 1981 and Tonya was walking through Stuyvesant Park in Bedstuy, Brooklyn. After a long day of cutting classes in the very popular Boys and Girls High School, Tonya ran into Mr. Flashy himself sitting on a candy red motorcycle. Tonya was the fly girl who stayed in the hallways to show off her runway worthy outfits. After she passed him, he offered her a ride home and the rest was pretty much history. From that day on, everything was about her new boo, Will. If my father said the sky was red, then Tonya believed it. That was some dangerous kind of love. No thanks.

"Girl, your father was something else. He had another girlfriend that looked just like me. People thought that was my twin sister. Yup, her name was Stacey," she said while rolling her eyes. "She had finger waves just like me, and coco brown skin. Your papa was a Rolling Stone."

I tried to keep a straight face but honestly, I couldn't believe the audacity of my father. I guess he had a type.

"Wow mommy," I replied, trying to stay neutral.

So back at the house, dad and myself sat down on the couch searching for things to say. A lot of things had happened in eleven years. I'm sure he was glad when his phone started to ring and it broke the silence. He abruptly stood up and said, "I have to go."

"OK pops," I said, trying to hide the disappointment.

I walked him down the three flights of steps while he explained his flight info for the next day. "Baby girl, I have an early flight at 7 AM in the morning. I wish I could stay longer."

I simply nodded in agreement. He was moving more than 3,000 miles away. I did appreciate his wife at the time for attempting to make a new life for him. I must admit she has weathered many storms with my dad. Out of their marriage came my beautiful sister, who is a teenager now. Our relationship hasn't been perfect; however, I want nothing more than to be a fun supportive sister to her.

I will admit, growing up I had a lot of animosity towards my sister. She wanted a relationship with me while I had bottled up resentment towards her that she knew nothing about. The pain I felt from the age of three clouded my adult mind. I was now a confused adult with manifested anger towards my little sister. She had no clue I cried and prayed to God many nights for the perfect lifestyle I thought she was living. My sister was half my age and didn't deserve me operating from a jealous ungodly place. I repented to God and asked for healing. If I had taken the time to get to know my sister, I would have found out her life wasn't ideal. The other side wasn't so green. Just like me, she was suffering too. My father's problems were manifesting in her life as well. Be careful what you wish for. My father's visit opened deep scars that I tried to bury.

As I get older, I have become more compassionate. I'm no longer looking at things with a natural eye. I want God's understanding of everything. God has granted me insight and a clean heart to forgive. I've learned that it wasn't my dad's fault. If he had control over the situation, I'm sure he would have changed the circumstances.

I pray for him and his well-being. I know the enemy tried to attack his destiny. However,

My God is bigger than all the above.

Today my relationship is better with my father. We don't speak that often, however we keep tabs on each other through Facebook and text messages. I'll randomly send him funny things to his inbox and vice versa. Acceptance is key. We can't change people.

God will fix them in his own timing. Until then, enjoy the moments you can. Holding on to grudges will only hinder you and your progress. The lessons, heartaches, and trails were all for a reason.

I'm not afraid to tell people my truth because it will help others. I can equally relate to the broken child and the adult who wants to heal from past trauma. God willing, many people will be healed through my truth.

Today I am thankful that I no longer carry animosity towards my father. My father almost lost his life recently from old habits. It took him almost dying for me to realize I had so much to say to him. I thank God for saving his life and allowing him a new chance to be a better man and father. Love you Pops!

Dear Father's,

Dust yourself off. You are not your mistakes. I know society has portrayed you as the enemy. However, let's show them how loving and merciful our God is. Please make decisions with your children's future in mind. Children should not have to suffer from your mistakes. Your children need you to show them how real men operate. You set the mark in their life concerning love and hope. Don't take your role lightly. We honor and value your presence. The Bible states in Proverbs 22:6:

"Start children off on the way they should go, and even when they are old, they will not turn from it." You are kings who have the privilege of raising young kings and queens. Let's learn from our mistakes and create families; not just one parent households. Let's vow to create a better tomorrow!

Signed,

A Daughter

Tonekia Williams

Pretty Girl Lost

But the lord stood by me and strengthened me, so that through me the message might be fully proclaimed, and all the gentiles might hear it. So I was rescued through the lion's mouth. Timothy 4:17

The little peace I had in life was going downhill fast. In other words, I was about to start going "buck wild." I kept wondering why my breast was so tender while on my girls' trip for my birthday. People knew me for being snappy, but I was extra mean for no reason. What a coincidence! I knew something was off about my body. Was I ready to be someone's mom? Once I got back from my trip, I rushed to the local pharmacy to confirm what I had already thought. When I asked Kenny if he was ready to be a daddy, he shook his head and told me, "Whatever you want to do is cool." Therefore, I repented to God in advance and went forth. I still wonder what my child would have looked like and how their personality would have been. The enemy tried to taunt me for years due to my decision. Now I can boldly say Jesus already died for ALL of my sins to be cleared. Whether past, future, or current mistakes, I am covered by the blood of Jesus. Not today, Satan! God heard my cries; never will I walk in shame again.

After the death of my grandmother, my family and I had gone through a total transformation. I'm sure gramma was turning in her grave at how we were behaving. The tight-knit family that she raised wasn't walking in love. In happier times, our house represented unity. When family and friends we're invited, they ate, laughed, cracked jokes, and came as they were pleased. As you climbed up the three flights of stairs, the smell of her chicken and dumplings, collard greens, and cornbread would slap you across your nostrils. Something was always manifesting in Clatis's oven or on top of her stove. Gramma expressed her love for her family through cooking. Her very own unique art. On good days, we would sit at the table while eating and discuss the fruits of our day. Well, after we thanked God and asked him to bless our food. The days we didn't sit at the table, I begged my gramma to keep the routine going.

"Gramma, could we sit at the table like the Cosby's?"

I would ask her in my most annoying voice. She would laugh and give in to my request. Oh how times had changed. Nowadays, when you walked through her threshold, it reeked of stale Newport's, confusion, Alize, and reefer. For all you new schoolers, reefer is weed. My family literally fell apart right before my eyes. Within a year, one of my aunts was evicted from her apartment and was forced to live with me. While my second aunt battled with mental insanity, the loss of her mom was too much for her to handle. Lastly, my mother started using alcohol and drugs as often as she could as her way of escape.

Wait, how could I forget my older cousin Nelle? After years of being clean from crack, she started using again to help her cope with my grandmother's passing. After years of battling her addiction, she lost places to run to. My grandmother never closed her door for her. That's why she took it so hard when she died. As for myself, I started seeking attention in all the wrong places, mainly from the opposite sex. God, why us? I asked more than any other question. Eventually the pressure became too much. I just wanted to leave my childhood neighborhood and start a new beginning. As soon as the opportunity appeared, I ran and didn't look back.

I ended up leaving everything I knew and went to stay with a good friend who I called my cousin. She had just got a new apartment near Pitkin Avenue in East NY, Brooklyn. That was the other side of Brooklyn and that wasn't for the weak. I guess the gentrification sweep missed that area. Cause baby!!! If you didn't have a heart, you did not belong in the area. The reputation for East New York wasn't so appealing. Yet, I loved it there. I was close to all my favorite cheap yet chic clothing stores. Anyone who knows me, knows I am a pretty frugal woman. Still, I adore fashion, follow trends, and set some of my own. With that being said, I would take $100 and go to Pitkin Avenue and splurge! I would walk right out of those cheap stores as if I was on Fashion Avenue in Manhattan. Can I get an Amen? Okay!

I lived with my childhood friend for about a year. I was used to living with my grandmother and being spoiled, but I had to make do with the opportunity I was given. Obstacle after obstacle started to present themselves. After sleeping on my friend's couch for about six months, my mom started to spiral out of control with her addictions. She was a completely different person. There was so much unmanageable pain in her and when speaking about her mom, she couldn't get through a full sentence without crying. In all honesty, no one was able to stay completely sane without gramma. My mom and her long-time hubby were starting to argue more and more due to stress and tension. After they had their love and war sessions, my mom would always end up getting kicked out and had nowhere to go. The most random late-night calls always woke me up out of my sleep. I suffered from bad anxiety growing up due to my mom and her reckless behavior. I never knew the last time I would see or speak to her. When my phone rang late at night, I anticipated a horrific story about my mom. On this particular night, she was crying.

"Tee where are you?" she asked in a pouty childlike way.

I replied as I was half asleep, "In the house ma, you ok?"

She got silent and then I could hear sniffling.

"Hello," I said, clearing my throat. Now the anxiety was kicking in.

"Mommy what's the matter?" The four-year-old protective little girl started to arise.

"I'm outside," she said.

"Ma, it's 4 AM, you should be in bed," I replied.

"I can't go home. He's going to hit me and I'm scared."

I was on my friend's couch, wishing I had my own space for my mother to come and spend the night with me. I wanted to protect my mommy. I needed her to be warm and safe with me. At 4 AM in Brooklyn, there were only pimps, prostitutes, murderers, and the mentally insane lurking outside. I refused to let that conversation be the last time I spoke to my mother. The protector in me suddenly kicked in.

"Ma, I'm calling you a cab now. Tell me the block you're on."

I hung up the phone and debated how I would tell my friend my mother was also coming over to sleep on the couch with me. When my mother finally arrived, her face was swollen, and she looked as if she was ready to throw in the towel.

Long story short, my mother stayed there with us for about a month. She didn't have any place to go. It was hard but we made it work. Eventually, she and her hubby reconnected and moved down south. With my mom living at my friend's house with me, it created an additional strain on our friendship. I understood it wasn't my friend's responsibility to provide shelter for myself and my mom. I was torn.

One thing about God, He heals and makes a way! Nehemiah 8:10 declares, "Do not grieve, for the joy of the Lord is your strength." I knew the situation was temporary and God was slowly making a way. I've noticed that God has a tricky way of allowing things to expire in your life for his divine purpose. Have faith.

You may not understand it at this moment but he's working it all out for you. Give it time. After four years of working what I thought was the perfect job, I was laid off. Maybe it was a blessing, but I gained about 40 pounds sitting around answering phones for 70% of the day. When I left work, I would literally cut my phone off. I'm appreciative of the opportunity, however it wasn't fulfilling. I wasn't reaching my full potential there. I knew outside of that job greatness awaited. I'm thankful I didn't stay and miss out on the experiences God had for me. I could've easily relied on being at that job for twenty plus years of my life, getting a secured check every two weeks, and retiring between the ages of forty and forty-five. The security of that job would have kept me bound. God had other plans for my life. He knew I was comfortable and wouldn't leave on my own. Therefore, the master took absolute control. Romans 8:28 quotes, "And we know that in all things

God works for the good of those who love him, who have been called according to his purpose."

In the blink of an eye, I was jobless and officially on my own without my granmma. Things weren't going the way I had imagined they would be, yet I was raised by some of the toughest women I knew. I pulled my big girl panties up and kept it moving. After a couple of months, I started working at a local daycare. It was a huge downgrade as far as pay was concerned; however, it was a humbling experience. It taught me to appreciate everything and make the best of what I had. During my time of grieving, I always knew God was in control. Even though I hadn't been to church in years I still had his word tattooed in my heart. Teaching children was always a passion of mine. I knew in the future I would be working with kids. The career shift was needed; weirdly it was working in my favor. I worked long days at the daycare from 7 AM to 6 PM with barely any breaks. Mr. Moshe, the owner, had a policy where he didn't allow his staff to leave the premises on their lunch breaks. I endured his antics because the job was off the books, which allowed me other opportunities. I enjoyed myself most of the time because we had fun at work. Tilly and I, a co-worker, became close friends. We would literally crack jokes all day between caring for the kids. We built such a great friendship and had so much in common.

In the mornings we understood there wouldn't be much dialogue between us. Both of us weren't morning people and opted not to speak until about 10ish. We taught our kiddos the fundamentals, then before we knew it, it was nap time at 12 PM. That was the absolute best part of the day. We fed our babies and then put them to sleep on their soft blue cots. All seven of those angelic faces would go right to sleep. Those cots provided the best sleep. Don't ask me how I know. We had our hands full most of the day. However, every day was a blessing because Tilly and I had each other. Thankful for my friend!

After a few months, I left my friend's house and rented a room from one of Tilly's associates. It seemed like I had gone from bad to worse. I was grateful to have my own space, but it came with repercussions. This was the most active and dangerous family I had ever met. They were neck and neck with my crazy family. Wow.

The room I was renting was huge with great lighting. Yet, there was always so much darkness in the home. My very first week there, I witnessed two incidents. All I can recall is hair pulling, bloody faces, lots of curses, and crying children. I prayed to God on a regular basis. "Please father allow me to be comfortable on this journey. I know I won't be here long. Make a way for me Lord."

It took about a year, then BOOM! Tilly had another hookup. She knew someone who was renting a studio down the block from the daycare. Finally, I officially was moving to an apartment of my own. No sharing. Praise the Lord! I was leaving the WWF wrestling match. The first day I moved in, it was bittersweet. I knew granmma was proud of me and smiling down from heaven.

It took me about two hours to unpack my things for my bedroom. It was time to make my place nice and comfy for my first night there.

My cozy studio was starting to look like home. Once I finished, I sat on the kitchen floor in amazement. I begin to take everything in. I thanked God for the journey that led me to that very moment. It wasn't easy and it all started to sink in. Down rolled a warm tear on my cheek. That was gratefulness falling from my eyes. I smiled and whispered, *"Thank you God."* After having several minutes of worship, I decided to cut my alarm clock radio on and listen to some music. Until I got a new radio, my family dollar alarm clock would play my tunes.

Here I was on the kitchen floor with a glass of Berringer wine, listening to classic R&B tunes. 105.1 always played the hottest throwback music which made me reminisce. A familiar song started to play, and I screamed out loud, "Oh no they didn't just play my song," *Cause I Ain't Never Had Nobody Do Me Like You* by Bow wow and Ciara had just taken me back to memory lane. That song always brought me back to my high school days. I can laugh now, but those days had sis stressed out!

From a youngin, my weakness was always guys. I found myself in the weirdest scenarios all the time. I mean all the time. My heart was always being broken by someone's disrespectful son. I was convinced that I was cursed when it came to making the right decisions dealing with men. Little did I know, things would not get better any time soon. The joke was on me. That song made me think of Brandon.

Brandon was my high school sweetheart. I am literally rolling my eyes. He made me fall in love with him. We went to high school together where he made it his business to find me throughout the day and make sure I was good. He would come to my lunch table every day and chill with me the whole period. When school was over, he would walk me home or make his way to come sit on my stoop later on in the evening. When my grandmother got to know him, she allowed us to come sit on the couch and watch movies together. We were inseparable. That was my laughing partner and best friend.

Something else that we also had in common were our mothers. They were fighting a fight, but alcohol was winning. At times they embarrassed us, but we loved them dearly. Sometimes I feel as though I ruined our relationship. Brandon was a good guy but at the time, I didn't appreciate him. I devalued him in many different ways.

Brandon forgave me but never forgot that I thought he wasn't enough for me. Even though I didn't cheat on him, he didn't like my ways. It did hurt but I got over it about twenty years later. I just laughed so loud, but I'm serious. We went back and forth for most of our teenage and adulthood years. No matter who we were with, we always found our way back to one another. It was like a weird addiction. Yes, you can literally be addicted to a person. A few years ago, I found myself praying that I would come to my senses and move on with my life. The guilt, loyalty, and familiarity kept me hostage. It was toxic. I couldn't let go of him, but eventually I moved on. When God knew I was ready to walk into the new light that he created, things started to change.

While sitting on the floor in my new favorite room, I made a toast to myself. I had come really far. The hard work and discomfort paid off. After about ten minutes, I heard a knock on the door.

I hesitated then shouted, "Who is it?"

"Ronny," said an old crackling voice.

I swung open the door, "How may I help you?"

"Sorry to bother you," he said. By viewing his posture, he was astonished at the way I swung open the door. "Your music is loud and it's late dear."

Looking at my clock on my stove, I noticed it was all of 8 PM. Did I mention I was listening to an alarm clock radio?

"Ok sir, I'll be mindful of my music," I said through clenched teeth. Then, I politely closed the door. After security had left the building, I ran to my bed to get ready for work the next morning.

The day care was right around the corner from my new place, so I could literally roll out of bed and sleep-walk to work. I turned on my favorite morning show to catch a couple laughs right before

I took the quickest shower possible. After hitting the snooze button about four times, I had 17 minutes to shower, eat, get dressed, and walk around the corner. I headed towards the door grabbing my keys from my pocket and then I began to jog down the stairs. When I reached the last step, the same old man from the night before opened his door revealing his denim overalls.

"Good morning," he said, locking eyes with me.

"Hello. Good morning," I said nonchalantly.

"Be careful how you run down those stairs. You don't want to break them," he said along with a nervous laugh.

I lightly chuckled then walked out the door. I then knew Mr. Overalls was going to be a headache. I couldn't believe my ears. My hands were really full. While walking around the corner, I noticed a White tinted Range Rover following me. Come on now, I thought to myself. It was too early for all the shenanigans. I stopped to see if I knew the driver, but the face wasn't familiar.

"Hello beautiful," the driver screamed out, while rolling down his passenger window.

"Can I drive you to where you're going," he asked.

I shook my head no because I sure didn't want to end up on a milk cartoon. The truck was nice but not that nice.

"I'm ok," I replied.

"Well can I leave you with my number? We can hang out sometime," he said confidently.

"I'm good," I rebutted.

Then I made a beeline into the daycare. Mr. Moshe was peering out the window to see who was coming in the gate. I have never seen someone watch from a camera and the window at the same time. I was certain he was hiding from the FBI or something. He made me nervous. Something never sat right in my spirit about Mr. Moshe. It was probably the Holy Spirit warning me not to get too close. As soon as I walked in the building, I could hear his orthopedic shoes tapping down the stairs.

"Hello, how are you?" he said in his heavy African voice.

Not giving me a chance to respond, he started making requests before I took off my jacket.

"Can you please sweep, mop the floor, then go to the grocery store once it opens," he said all in one breath.

"Good morning Moshe," I said sarcastically.

"Sure," I said with clenched teeth.

Bear with me guys. God was still working on me at that time.

I finished my task then headed up the block to the grocery store. Guess who was in the store? Yup Mr. White Range Rover. I tried to act like I didn't see him, but he was in hot pursuit.

"I'm Darryl. What's your name, beautiful?"

I could hear a Caribbean accent sneaking out of his mouth. He then extended his hand.

"I'm Tee. Nice to meet you Darryl," I said while shaking his hand.

"Well you know this is meant to be right," he said.

"Umm, if you say so. I'm just here to get some groceries for my job," I said, revealing a fake smile.

We both laughed.

"Here, take my number please," extending his business card. "You live over here?" he asked.

I took the card out of his hand and put it in the back pocket of my blue denim jeggings.

"Yes, I recently moved around the corner," I replied way too fast, as if I knew this man personally.

"Oh ok, that's what's up. Do you need anything for your new place?" Darryl asked.

That question caught me by surprise. I then realized that it was 90 degrees and didn't have an AC or a TV yet. However, I shook my head and said "No."

He responded, "I don't believe that. I'm headed to Best Buy. Do you have an AC yet?"

Wow, did this man just read my mind?

"Well, honestly I don't have an AC yet, but I'm going to get one this weekend along with a TV."

He walked off.

"Okay no problem shortly. Make sure you text me, ok," he said walking away looking back smiling.

Darryl wasn't very handsome, but he had charm and was well-mannered. He stood about 5'7, brown skin, and stocky with a little belly.

Darryl kept walking while looking back, smiling. He probably had a trick up his sleeve.

When I got home that night something told me to text him, so I did.

The text said, "It's Tee, save my number."

He replied immediately. "Responding took you long enough. Where can I drop off this AC and TV? Its sitting in the back of my truck."

"Wow, I told you I was ok," I replied.

Deep down inside I was pleasantly surprised. Yet, I didn't want Darryl thinking I owed him anything.

He replied, "Send addy."

After about twenty mins, he arrived blasting "What We Do" by Beenie Seagle and Freeway. We sat in his truck talking for about an hour. He was actually fun to talk to and very sincere. I thanked him and told him I was very appreciative. I also told him not to get any ideas because I wasn't looking to date at the moment. I warned him I had a lot going on and dating wasn't important to me at the time. He reassured me that he just wanted to be my friend and get to know me. He brought my things up the stairs and told me he would text me when he got home. Of Course, Mr. Overalls was peeking out his blinds when we entered the gate. That man just wouldn't stop. After he dropped my gifts off, I started to prepare some jerk cheeseburgers while listening to a Beyonce YouTube mix.

After about two hours, I called Darryl to make sure he made it home ok. The phone rang out twice and then went to voicemail. Shortly after, I began to our a glass of wine to go with my juicy jerk burgers. Cooking and eating have always been my favorite pastimes. Haha.

When I was done, I showered and headed to club bed where DJ pillow was rocking all the latest hits. For some reason I tossed and turned all night. I didn't feel alone in the house. That was one of many sleepless nights. When my alarm clock went off in the morning, I wanted to cry. I snoozed for about ten mins then dragged myself out of bed. I didn't receive any calls or texts from my new buddy Darryl, which I thought was strange. I hoped he was ok.

While walking around the corner to work, I blasted *"Trouble Don't Last Always"* by Rev Timothy Wright. Whenever I wanted to feel close to my granmma and get comfort, I listened to that song. He may not come when you want him, but he's on timmmmeee!! Those were the lyrics and I felt that in my soul because it was the truth. I envisioned gramma frying chicken wings while blasting that song. As I got closer to the daycare, my phone began to ring. It was a private caller. I almost didn't answer, but then I thought it could've possibly been an emergency.

"Hellooo," I basically sang out.

I was in a pretty decent mood after I listened to my early morning motivation. The person on the other end listened for about ten seconds then I heard a female voice begin to speak.

"Hi, is this Tee?"? The voice was actually a polite one.

Wait, this can't be a bill collector this early, I thought to myself.

I answered, "How can I help you?"

"This is Darryl's wife. I see that you two have been texting and calling his phone."

Her words dropped like Funk Master Flex bombs.

"Wow," I replied. "You have absolutely nothing to worry about Ms. I can assure you I don't want your husband. I actually want my own husband one day. I'm not trying to block my blessings. Have a blessed day," I stated. Then I ended the call and walked into my job.

The audacity of Mr. Darryl. When I walked into the daycare, just like most days, Moshe was waiting near the entrance with a to-do list.

"Hi, can you—" I stopped him in mid- sentence.

"Morning Moshe. Please allow me to put my things down."

I then proceeded to run up the wooden stairs straight to the adult restroom. As soon as I reached the stall, I had no shame. I dropped to my knees and repented to God.

"God, I'm sorry. I didn't know he was married."

One thing God doesn't play with is adultery. Hebrews 13:4 states, "Let marriage be held in honor among all, and let the marriage bed be undefiled, for God will judge the sexually immoral and adulterous." I knew God would forgive me because Jesus had already died for my sins. I wanted to let God know I was sorry. Now the next issue was should I give away my gifts. I figured those were ok to keep. As I walked around and got familiar with my new neighborhood, it amazed me how many churches were in such close proximity. There was a church on every other corner. The last time I had been to church was many moons ago. After Gramma was diagnosed with cancer, she became ill and wasn't very mobile. Church was kind of put on the back burner for me. God however was still in my heart. On my way home from work one summer evening, I could hear gospel music and smell burning franks in the air. Now that was my type of party. Everyone who is familiar with me knows how much I love grilled food. I crossed the street and saw a group of churchgoers lifting their voices to *Every Praise* by Hezikiah Walker. "Every praise is to our God, Every word of worship in one accord. Every praise, every praise is to our God." They sounded amazing. Their voices captivated me more than the smell of those hot dogs. I slowed down but something in me wanted to come to a complete stop. My arm reached out and grabbed a pamphlet from a tall dark man who was passing them out. "Come Join us sis," he said in a heavy Jamaican accent. I told him I had to go home and would join them for a Sunday service soon. Eventually God led me there.

Double G

No temptation has overtaken you except what is common to mankind. And God is faithful; he will not let you be tempted beyond what you can bear. But when you are tempted, he will also provide a way out so that you can endure it.

1 Corinthians 10:13

It was one of the hottest days of the year and going outside was the last thing on my mind. I remember being up the night before really late after having terrible nightmares. It was the second night I had woken up with strange bruises on me. I would always say to myself, "I guess I was fighting in my dreams". I would immediately drop to my knees and began to pray for protection. I would also pray against any demonic issues that may have taken place while I was sleep. Deep down I knew there was something happening to me that always left me lost for words. Starting at such a young age, there were always mysterious occurrences. Most of the experiences I went through growing up can't be put into words. From sleepwalking as a young girl to sexually experimenting from a young age. It also made me upset that I would always hear and see things no one else saw. Sharing my experiences with others seemed impossible. What would people think of me? I vowed most of my secrets would go to the grave right along with me. That's until I became free.

After decades, the yolk has been broken. All Glory to God. From observation and experience, I've noticed that the enemy attempts to plant seeds in the minds of young children. Seeds of lust, negativity, perversion, grief, embarrassment, and all things shameful and ungodly. I remember being as young as four years old, having perverse thoughts. At that tender age, what did I know? Demonic spirits had obviously taken over my household and found their way inside of my thoughts and actions. While everyone was asleep, I would make my way on my grandmother's tall piano and climb to the very top. I would then open the window and climb outside onto the fire escape. Yup, I was still four. I would sit out there and watch the strange people walking up and down the block scheming for their next hit of drugs. When done, I would climb right back in bed with gramma. Only God knew what was going on in my mind!

My neighborhood was one of the most drug-infested areas in Brooklyn. In the early 90's, crack was wrecking homes and families. So many adults my age are still recovering from the effects of the crack era. Only by the grace of God am I still living and breathing. I could have easily fallen off that fire escape and broken all my little bones while my family were asleep. I can also remember many times waking up in the middle of the night and seeing weird shadows standing over me and my grandmother. To be so young, my braveness still surprises me. I would not tell my family until the next morning the things I saw at night.

I would say, "Gramma, last night there were three men standing over us in long white gowns and their heads were covered with white scarves." She would laugh it off but deep down I'm sure she knew I was different. I encourage the parents who will read this book to teach your children how to pray at a young age. Always keep open dialogue with them because you want to create an environment where they feel safe speaking to you about all things. The enemy comes at a young age to kill, steal, and destroy what God has already planned for our lives. He wants to steal legacies and end lives at very young ages. Keep your children constantly covered in prayer. Keep your environment pure and healthy for your children's sake. Spirits do not discriminate.

I walked to the shower as I was surprised at how much energy I still had. Surprisingly, I was running on less than three hours of sleep. The artist Prince always came to mind when I needed some gas in my tank. "If I was your girlfriend, I'd be there for you. If somebody hurt you, even if that somebody was meee meeeeee." Prince always did it for me. My aunt Sheryl was responsible for turning me on to old school music. I can remember at six holding a brush up to my mouth mouthing the words of Prince and Barry White. Today, I am still a lover of old school music.

Besides Gospel, Old School R&B is my go-to music. Now don't get me wrong, there are some amazing new school artists. However, how could you hold a grudge with your partner if he played some Babyface, Al Green, Stevie Wonder, or Curtis Mayfield? I'll answer my own question. You can't! I loved spending the nights at Auntie Sheryl's house. She didn't have any children of her own so my cousins and I were spoiled rotten. Auntie called me her Snotty-booger until I was about twenty-six. Yuck.

When I went to her apartment on East 92 in Brownsville Brooklyn on the weekends, I didn't want to come home. I never left empty handed. In the summer, my uncle V and my aunt would take me to Great Adventure's as well as to the coolest water parks. They were such a fun couple. So many people had admiration for them. Most of the time, I wished they were my parents. Uncle Vernon was my aunt's common law husband. They had dated since they were young. They were high school sweethearts. When they finally decided to get married, Aunt GG was crushed when she found out some devastating news. Someone had already used her name fraudulently to get married. Sheryl and Vernon were everyone's ideal couple. They traveled the world together, laughed, joked, and never seemed like they had dull moments. Still, everyone knew my aunt wore the pants in the relationship, except Vernon. Yet he rolled with the punches. I don't think I ever saw him get angry. Vernon was a NYC bus driver who worked long hours to bring home the bacon. In return, GG fried, smothered, baked, or broiled that little piggy. My aunt had many warm characteristics. She was loyal, loving, caring, and went to no ends to help her family succeed. However, being headstrong and controlling were some of her negative traits.

My family learned to tolerate her domineering ways and we counted it off as her being the oldest. We knew in a weird way she meant well. On the other hand, after more than a decade, Vernon decided he wanted to lead his own life. One day while GG was at work, he packed all of his things and moved out of the house they shared. When my aunt returned home from work, she was greeted by a half empty house. Vernon had changed his number and moved on with his life. After the bills became too overwhelming, Sheryl was forced to move. To her convenience, a vacant apartment in the same building as her mother was available. GG lived on the first floor while I and Gramma lived on the 4th. It was nice having her close to us while she was going through such a devastating time in her life. While she laughed and smiled, you could tell there was emptiness inside. My aunt was going through such a tragic time.

After my grandmother's death, my aunt's mental sanity started to decline. My sweet gramma was my aunt's best and possibly only friend. No one understood her like her mama. I often cracked jokes, but it was the truth; gramma raised all of us to be antisocial. None of us had a lot of friends; only one another. When all failed, we could always depend on family. As I got older, many things changed. I was able to make my own decisions and deal with my family by choice. Most of the days, I couldn't connect with my aunt, which gave me anxiety when she came around. When I moved, I stayed away for long periods of time. Deep down I knew this wasn't a wise decision. I wanted to be there for her, but a weird presence always lingered when she was around. I promised myself when June came around, we would celebrate her birthday together. I told her not to make any plans because I was making it my business to take her to her favorite seafood restaurant, Red Lobster. It was something so surreal about our time together that day. She shared so much wisdom and insight on life during our conversation. I had never felt close to her. This day she was so understanding and relatable. There wasn't any judgement; only uncut, heart-to-heart girl talk. That day we laughed and almost cried at how much we were missing granmma. Time had flown by. Year three of grandma's death was approaching. If only I had known that would be the last birthday I would spend with my aunty, I would have shared so much more, hugged her 1000 times, and told her I love her to infinity. Life is really short. Love your family members beyond their mistakes.

While speaking to my aunt that day at dinner, I noticed the many multicolored small beads around her neck. When I asked her what they were for, she told me she wore them for protection. I didn't ask any more questions. I figured they served the same purpose of the many statues around her house and over her door. For years I noticed my aunt had weird stuff around her apartment, but I never did any research on what she was practicing. If I would have done my homework, things would have made more sense. Her life and my family's lives were affected because certain lifestyles come with a huge price. Sadly, the price she paid was her life. After we ate our endless shrimp and biscuits, I walked her to the bus stop before we went our separate ways.

In the morning I woke up feeling a little annoyed. Not sure if I had a bad dream or if it was that time of the month. While walking to work, something told me to reach out to my aunt Sheryl. I called and got the voicemail. It was full. The next day, which was Friday, my phone rang and it was GG. She was insisting that I come over and chill with her for the night. I didn't plan on coming back outside once I got home. However, her offering to treat me to seafood changed my mind real quick. I jumped out of bed and into my black tights, white v neck shirt, and black converse sneakers. Once I got there, I noticed how bad my aunt was doing. I had to walk sideways to get into her house. She had clothes, shoes, and other personal items stacked to almost the ceiling. My poor aunty was hoarding her personal belongings to the point that she could barely walk in her house. This made me feel guilty that I wasn't around to help her. Life lesson. No matter how strong people may appear to be, we all need a shoulder to cry on. My aunt was suffering from depression and hoarding, amongst other things. For the rest of the night, we talked, laughed, and ate our tasty seafood. We had another night of enjoying each other's company. This was twice in one week. I figured it was going to snow in June. When it got late, I decided to call a cab and head back home.

While in the cab headed there, I had received a text from Brandon. Before I opened the text, I rolled my eyes as I kept going back to my promises to myself. After all these years, why couldn't I leave this man alone? After a few moments I gave in and opened the text. It read "WYD." Brandon was a bad habit that I was trying to kick. We often went for long periods of time without speaking. Yet, we always found our way back to each other. I counted to twenty, then nonchalantly texted back, "Nothing much, what's up?" After a few more texts, he was at my house before the cab got there.

After embracing each other and smiling until our cheeks hurt, we drove to Popeyes. When we arrived, I got my favorite chicken tenders and dirty rice. Afterwards we laughed in the car like kids for about two hours. We always had a routine when the time ended for us to hang out. We would hug goodbye and I would tell him to text me when he got home. He would nod his head in agreement, but he would never start his car. Once I stepped inside my house, his text would come like clockwork. He would send a pair of eyes and it was a done deal after that. Monday always came way too soon.

After I checked the news, I surely wasn't excited about the field trip that was planned for the day. It was going to be 95 degrees, yet Moshe had a bright idea to take the kids to Coney Island.

Coney Island is an amusement park in Brooklyn that happens to be by a beach. There is absolutely no shade there. Don't get me wrong, I enjoyed taking the children on field trips that allowed them to partake in new adventures. However, the heat that day dampened my mood.

It felt like "deja vu "when my mother called while I was on the trip with the kids. She asked if I had spoken to my Aunt GG. I replied, "No ma, I'll call you when I get home." I was hot and frustrated, but I knew my mom was on worry mode. When we left the amusement park, we decided to take the kiddies to McDonalds for ice cream and french fries as a treat. I stepped away to go to the bathroom and while walking, my phone started ringing again. I answered as soon as I stepped in the stall. My mother was on the other end of the line hysterically crying. I could barely make out what she was saying. All I heard was the smell and your aunty. It took her a few minutes, but she finally told me between sobs, that my aunt was found dead in her apartment. She had suffered from a heart attack and had been there for two days. That meant she died the night I saw her. Someone had reported a foul smell coming from her apartment. In less than three years, two of my family members were found dead in the same apartment building. My mother had ignited both findings. After a while, my co-worker came inside the bathroom to see what was taking me so long. She found me crying on the dirty public restroom floor.

"Lord, why us?" is what I kept repeating in my head.

I couldn't understand why this was happening to us. We had suffered way too much and for so long. We were all tired. RIP AUNT GG. You are loved and missed!

While living at my new place, I noticed there were always strange things going on. For example, the television cut on by itself, things dropped in other rooms, and it was just a feeling of not being alone even though I was. My nightmares also intensified once my aunt died. I can vividly remember waking up several nights not being able to move. For the record, that is one of the scariest times ever. The elders would call this being ridden by the witch. The scientific term provided by google is sleep paralysis. It is a state, during waking up or falling asleep, in which a person is aware but unable to move or speak. Talking about scary? Yes, imagine that you're attempting to wake up out of your sleep but you can't move. No matter how hard you would try, it felt as if something was holding you down. Sometimes, I could hear strange voices. I have suffered many nights since I was a small child with these attacks. I started to do lots of research and then God blessed me with a good friend who was experiencing the same trauma. Together we did lots of studying, fasting, and detoxing. By the grace of God, things started to get better. I believe I was experiencing hardships so I would be able to help others down the line.

On different occasions I would wake up to the strangest bruises and cuts on me. How could I explain these shocking experiences when I didn't have answers for myself? I refused to tell people because I thought they would think I was nuts. So here I am, living alone, having nightmares, feeling like someone was smothering me, and then waking up to seeing fresh bruises and cuts on myself. What a timeline!! I got the courage and started sharing my issues with a couple of people whom I trusted. I was told I should get some sage, frankincense, and a dream catcher from the local spiritual store. Every item I purchased appeared to make the attacks increase. I was lost and confused. Yet I tried to stay in good spirits. No one knew what I was dealing with behind closed doors and I didn't understand myself. One Sunday, I got up really early. I declared this was the Sunday I would rededicate my life to God and start going back to church. I got dressed and made my way down the block and around the corner to the big white church that captured me that day with the grilled food. When I walked in, I felt like all eyes were on me. Some of the women were welcoming and some women gave me the once over from head to toe. However, I was as warm and friendly as I normally am. I noticed a couple of men giving me the eye but I quickly turned the other cheek. They both had wives. When the Bishop preached, I identified with him. His sermons were short and sweet with lots of motivation in between. He kept his congregation laughing and wide awake. In my mind this was the uncle who made everyone laugh at the dinner table at Thanksgiving. I often imagined what it would be like to be a part of his family. I went to this church for seven years, sitting in the same row with the same people.

However, when I left, I still felt an empty void which made me go home to fulfill them with my same old sins. Maybe that's the reason I never joined the church. Only God knows that answer or where he intended for me to go. My church experiences were fulfilling for those moments. When I returned home, the same dreams, visions, and unexplainable things were still taking place and I was not taking my walk seriously. I was still in the club, drinking, fornicating, and not reading my bible at all. Many churchgoers partially serve God and I was guilty of this. We want to serve and be delivered on Sundays yet go back to the same thing we are being delivered from after church. God wants our full attention. Living holy is a lifestyle. We have to constantly set an environment for God to dwell in. For whoever would save his life will lose it, but whoever loses his life for my sake will find it according to Matthew16:25. We must constantly die to our flesh. No, we aren't expected to be a perfect people; only our Father in heaven is perfect. Yet every day we should strive to be better than we were the day before.

One day after a long 11-hour shift with my kiddies, something just didn't feel right in my spirit. When I left the daycare, I never went back. Was that the brightest decision? Nope. Did I have another job lined up? Nope. I just wasn't able to get any time off, so I knew I wouldn't be able to land an interview and move forward.

I was moving off emotion and it resulted in a lot of problems, stress, and debt. It took me about three months to start working at another job. During the waiting process, I was faced with depression and suicidal thoughts. The enemy was playing with my mind. I even reached out to Moshe, asking for my job back. He declined. That probably was a blessing.

I continued going to church and kept my faith in God. After getting two separate referrals from two different friends, I applied at a company that housed intellectually disabled people. This wasn't an ideal company and they had such a bad reputation. After working there for four years, I understood why. However, the love for the clients kept me there longer than expected. Their hiring process was also quick. After the first day of orientation, I knew what to expect. The instructors were using slang and watching all the women from head to toe. The class was loud and rowdy but I didn't care much. I knew it was a steppingstone and would allow me to pay my rent and buy groceries. With not much in between, I was a person who didn't mind working hard with two or three jobs. My friends joked and called me a Jamaican, referring to their strong work ethic. They would say, "Wow Tee, how many jobs do you need? You work hard girl." I would laugh, but it was true. I was the product of some really hard-working women. If we wanted something, we worked hard and then went to claim it.

The first day on the job I was petrified. The training scared me. It seemed as if they were preparing us for battle. The adults in our care ranged from nineteen to seventy. Every client had a different story, background, and diagnosis. Most of them had been in the system since they were children. A couple of the patients had come from Willowbrook State Institution. Willowbrook State School was a state-supported institution for children with intellectual disabilities located in Staten Island from 1947 until 1987. The children there were subjected to many hardships like being malnourished, physically abused, and deprived of proper medication. Most children were abandoned by their families. The system that was put in place to protect the kids failed them miserably.

As I walked in the front door of the facility in Harlem, New York, I could smell fear and Lysol. It also was accompanied by this weird stench that smelled like drool. All I knew was that every house I worked in had the same exact smell. I signed this huge red book and left my initials. Someone named Tante escorted me around the house. She was the assistant manager, a tall heavy-set woman with long cornrows. You could tell Tante didn't play any games; however, she was sweet. As I walked through the facility, I noticed there were many holes in the walls. We walked down a long hallway that had the brightest yellow walls that led to the kitchen. I was reaching for the kitchen when I heard a low muffled voice say hello. I turned around and noticed a man standing behind me with a shirt full of holes. When I looked down, he had one sneaker on. I waved hello and asked him what his name was.

"Daniel," he whispered.

"Nice to meet you Daniel," I replied.

When I finally reached the kitchen there were chairs thrown all over the place. Chicken, rice, salad, and plates were also thrown to the floor. I then saw someone run past me in their underwear. That was Daniel. Things unraveled in less than ten minutes. I honestly wanted to go back home, but something told me things would get better. As the day grew shorter, the house died down.

There were four women and five men. The 4 -12 shift was the busiest. Thank God for good staff and eventually we stuck together like a big family and that included our clients. We made sure the clients ate healthy meals and received their medication twice a day. After medication every night about 9 PM, it was bedtime. That's when the staff was finally able to let their hair down and they did just that. We would have some of the most intense conversations. The company that hired me was constantly bringing new people. Therefore, the house was filled with all types of people. If I ever become president, direct care workers will get their own holiday. These people wear many hats and risk their lives taking care of the intellectually disabled. Yet their pay does not reflect the effort they put in. Shout out to you guys!! Whoop whoop!

I would get home about 2AM every morning. There wasn't much excitement in my life but work, clients, and home. God was taking me through many avenues in preparation for my calling. I was fully aware this was all God's plan.

Insecure

And let steadfastness have its full effect, that you may be perfect and complete, lacking in nothing. James 1:4

It took me many years to recognize my worth. The enemy tries to rob you of the many tools God has given you to succeed in life. Many things held me back from having confidence in myself, on the outside I was a trendy woman. Deep inside, I was wounded from years of hurt. Why do we choose to walk in shame and belittle ourselves? I know now that the decisions I was making were coming from such a broken place. Most of the relationships I was involved in were very toxic. I was not respecting myself or my boundaries. I was attempting to be a people pleaser when I should have been pleasing God. I noticed I was lonely even though I had a host of friends and associates. I was the life of the party and most people enjoyed my company. Margaritas, Ciroc, and wine were my best friends. Drinking kept my mind at ease when people became too much for me. I suffered terribly from social anxiety. My definition for social anxiety is the fear of being judged in social situations. I hated public speaking, networking, and making new friends. Being in those environments worried me. I would always wonder what people were thinking of me. To alleviate my mind from running wild, I would show up drunk to events. I was dependent on liquor to give me courage and personality. It calmed my nerves and allowed me to fit in. I didn't go anywhere without my two small nips of white liquor. They were usually poured inside an orange or lemonade juice drink. I had to pray to be delivered from that drinking demon or it could have ruined my life. I was stagnating my own growth and aligning myself with failure. But let me tell you guys and gals something: PRAYER WORKS. Even through the stagnation, I always knew I would become a business owner, an author, a homeowner—and the list doesn't stop there. When you serve an amazing God, he does not put any limitations on his children. He will birth you with ideas and provide you with the resources to be successful.

Insecurities will have you bound in darkness. I noticed that God was allowing me to continue to go in circular motions until I had learned my lesson. My mother had suffered from alcohol abuse most of her life and here the enemy was trying to lead me down the same generational road. During my self-care transition, I noticed a few things about myself.

I kept attracting broken people because I was broken myself. I wasn't living up to my full potential, so I started dating people with the same type of problems that I had. How could two people headed for destruction help each other? My relationships, friendships, and decisions reflected my opinion of myself. Are you maintaining healthy relationships? If not, try your best to evaluate yourself and the people who surround you. Some situations can be avoided if we put our self-desires to the side and focus on living righteously. It may sound corny, however, when I'm in doubt about something I'm doing, I think to myself, would God approve of this? It works every time!

Every day I headed to work, I had no idea what would take place. The clients and staff were unpredictable. Even though we were this huge blended family, everyone had their off days. On a particular day I walked in the house and noticed that my manager was standing in the hallway, leaning on those bright yellow walls. I could always tell when something was bothering her. I wasn't sure if it was her work life or personal life. There was something about Ms. Knight that I gravitated to. I always had a soft spot for the misunderstood. None of the staff liked her, but I knew she didn't mean any harm. She had a good heart, but most people didn't want to see past her hard exterior. Ms. Knight was married but didn't have any biological children. The late nights that she stayed at the facility was an indication there wasn't much happiness at home.

"Hello Ms. Knight," I said to her and smiled.

She smiled back and that was rare. "I was waiting for you to come. I need a favor."

I knew something was up with that smile.

"Okay what's the matter," I replied.

"Please take Lorena to the Bronx to see her mom. She's been misbehaving. I know she misses her family. It's been a while."

I agreed. How could I say no. Lorena was the youngest person there. Being twenty-one years old, I'm not sure how she lasted there with so many older people. Lorena suffered from many mental disorders; however, I knew love and attention would help her along the way. I always brought her treats and picked out her clothes the night before so she would look cute for school. That day we walked to the train station and jumped on the 1 train. In about forty minutes we had reached our destination. While on the train we had some girl talk, she spoke about missing her family, the cute boys at school, and the new Jordan's that we're coming out. Lorena enjoyed being out of the facility since all of the other clients were twice her age and non-verbal. When we got to her mother's house, I could see there was a little hesitation. I asked her if she still wanted to go inside and she nodded. After we caught our breath from the long flight of stairs, we knocked on the door. There, a pale heavyset Spanish woman answered.

"Hola," she said nonchalantly.

Lorena hugged and greeted her mom with excitement. I spoke to her mom briefly about her behavior at home and how happy she was to come visit. Lorena spoke to her in the kitchen quietly while I sat in the living room with Lorena's brother. He was also intellectually disabled. He kept passing me the remote. When I attempted to change the channel, he would snatch the remote back. After about thirty minutes of the same thing, I excused myself to go check on Lorena. I noticed she was crying when I went back. I rushed to her and asked if she was okay. She nodded and said she was ready to go. Quickly, I gathered my things and reported back to her. I tried to speak to her mom on our way out, but she brushed me off by saying, "Ok, ok, and goodnight now." We left and headed back down the dark hot stairwell. While outside, I asked Lorena if she wanted to talk about her visit. She looked at me and screamed. "No!" Her scream startled me, and I told her it was okay for her to be upset and we would talk when she was ready. Our ride home was silent. I knew she was hurting. When we got back, I had two more hours until it was time to go home. It was Friday and Saturday was my early day; working from 7 AM to 3 PM. As I escorted Lorena to get her medication, I received a text message from Kyle.

I met Kyle on Instagram, and because my page was public, one day he randomly started liking my pictures. I think he liked about ten pictures. He was trying to get my attention. I went back on his page to view his pictures and surprisingly he was adorable. He had the most beautiful brown eyes and from his page, I saw he was adventurous. He traveled a lot and had a love for seafood. I thought to myself, hey maybe we can be friends. He slid in my DM and we started to chat. He was funny and we instantly clicked. After about a month of texting and talking, Kyle was reaching out to hang with me. He wanted to get some seafood, drinks, and smoke some hookah. I was sold after the food and drinks. The day was long and I needed to unwind. I texted him my job address and he told me he would be there in thirty minutes.

I freshened up in the bathroom and patiently waited for him to come. Before I left, I did one last house check to make sure the clients were sleeping. I walked outside and he was playing *Let's Get Married* by Jagged Edge. I thought it was cute. He also got out of the car and opened the door like a gentleman. The night was starting off good. I loved how myself and Ky had real life chats. His mom was a recovering alcoholic and his father had abandoned him at a young age. We always talked about the hurt our parents had caused us and how we would make such great parents one day. While we were driving, he got an important call. He needed to head back home to grab something he forgot. We both decided to grab our food and drinks and head inside. He had hookah there as well so we would just hang out indoors. We grabbed our food and thought it was a cute idea to have an inside picnic. Instead of Hookah, he insisted we just smoke some weed. I agreed but deep down I knew it wasn't a good idea. A few years prior, I had a really bad experience. I was chilling with some friends and ate a weed brownie. Most people would have only eaten half of the brownie. Hence why most people don't have this story to tell.

Guys, let's just say it didn't end well. After I ate the brownie, I started hallucinating and spent the night in the hospital. I promised myself and God I would never deal with weed again. Yet here I was, trying not to disappoint someone. Instead, I ended up disappointing myself. I must have forgotten I was smoking weed that night and thought I was smoking hookah. Long story short, I ended up hallucinating again. The high from the weed lasted all night. I was paranoid to the point I thought the guy was trying to kill me with a remote under the pillow. Talk about embarrassing! I also couldn't make it home that night because I couldn't feel my legs. So once again, I had put myself in an uncomfortable situation. I could have easily gone back home to my own scary house.

The next day I was mandated to work at 7 AM. Still high and tired from the night before, I said my prayers before I walked in the building. I promised God that if he allowed me to keep my sanity I would never smoke again. He kept his promise, but I surely did smoke several times after that. I'm glad to serve a merciful father who gives many chances. The shift I worked that morning was the longest shift ever. I'm not sure how I was able to keep my job. I slept almost the whole six hours in the client's living room. We were honestly a family there and we all had each other's back. The next day was Sunday. I made it my business to go to church and praise the Lord. I felt extra thankful that day because I knew God had shown me mercy. A lot of people lost their minds over situations of that nature. While the choir was singing, I started to feel tingling in my body and I began to jump up and down uncontrollably. God was having his way with me. After the songs were finished, the Bishop started to pray. "Grab your neighbor's hands tightly and pray for them." Before I knew it, one of the women from the choir had made her way from behind the pulpit to come pray with me. As soon as she touched me, my eyes closed tightly, and I saw a beaming white light and started shaking. It was an out of body experience. Yes, it was hard to explain so when I did get home from church, I googled "seeing white lights while praying." As you can see, I was desperate to see what I was witnessing. Before I left church, I brought dinner from the kitchen. They usually sold food right after service. Those elders could really cook. After each meal, I joked to myself saying I was going back to shake the cooks' hands. I looked down at my plate and the turkey wing, mac and candied yams were completely demolished. After a long scorching shower, I put on my favorite pajamas and laid in bed. I was still in disbelief about my last 48 hours. I listened to some smooth grooves while I tried to get my mind right. I closed my eyes and envisioned me being on a deserted island with no worries, just the sound of the tides. There was no one to impress and no one to judge me. I craved to be problem free.

Money started to become a major issue, my bills and the low paying wages weren't in agreement. I started to come up short with my rent payments. The job I was working for wasn't paying much which left me depressed. The depression was followed by severe panic attacks. One minute, I would be talking to my family and then out of the blue, I would black out. They would last about five to ten seconds; while it was happening, I had no idea what was going on. After taking several trips to the doctor, I left there with no answers or treatment. I was told to get some rest or see a psychiatrist. That was a depression overload on top of everything else I was going through. I started applying for other jobs while doing my best to remain calm. After two months, I received a second job working with autistic adults in the morning. After my night shift, I was headed straight to the new job. I didn't get much rest, but I was able to pay some bills. After about a year of intensity, a nurse from my night job gave me a reference to start working for the NYC Department of Education. I was excited. I wanted to work for the DOE for many years. It was a great door opener. My horizons were broadened. God was always by my side even when I felt alone. After a few months, which seemed like the longest hiring process ever, it was finally over. My foot was in the door and I was able to learn and start developing my future. Nothing is impossible. You may feel like you're moving backwards but you're being prepared for greatness.

Tonekia Williams

"No Weapon Formed"

No weapon formed against you shall prosper. Isaiah 54:17

Note: This was several years later.

N o weapon formed against me shall prosper! No weapon formed against me shall prosper!!!" I chanted out loud about twenty times while on my knees with tears streaming from my face. I couldn't understand what was happening to me at that point and I felt like I was being punished. As scrambled thoughts entered my mind, the last thing I remembered was feeling weird after dinner laying in the bed next to Nathaniel. We always sat and ate while we discussed our day. Nathaniel had surprised me after work with such a good seafood meal. He knew my weakness. When I came through the door, he had everything set up so nice for me. Crab legs, shrimp, and mussels were my favorite dishes. We both had a thing for spoiling each other and there was a lot of competition in our relationship. Friendly cook offs and surprise planning was our love language. We argued like cats and dogs, but we literally could not stay away from each other. He was my peace after the storm, and it felt like I had literally gone through hell up until this very point.

After a shower, I laid next to Nate with my belly full, fuller than ever. I dozed off for about 30 minutes. When I woke up, I felt as though I couldn't move. Nate was sleeping so peacefully I chose not to disturb him. I tried to remain calm, slowly saying in my head, "No weapon formed against me shall prosper, no weapon formed against me shall prosper." That bible quote was my personal security and advocate. Actually, I love that scripture so much, I had it tattooed on my arm. When I was able to move, I jumped out of bed and landed on the floor. I felt like I was being attacked by something invisible. There was tingling in my face and my arms and my body felt so stiff. Nathaniel finally woke up and asked, "Are you okay?" He was trying to keep his cool while staring at me on the floor with my knees planted on the ground. The expression on his face was priceless. In my head, I knew this would be the last time he spent the night with me. Even though I was being attacked by the unknown, I tried to keep it cool, in hopes that I wouldn't freak him out too bad. The bible in my hands and scriptures in my mouth kept me company for about ten minutes. When the numbness died down, I ran to the bathroom and continued to pray vigorously. I was on my knees again but this time in front of the toilet. I recited every scripture I knew, hoping this would really get whatever was attacking me upset. Hebrews 4:12, "For the word of God is alive and active, sharper than any double-edged sword." Those scriptures were cutting up some stuff. I continued to pray and worship God while in the bathroom and after a while, I started to feel like my normal self. When I got back to the bed, I climbed in next to Nathaniel who was headed back to sleep. It surprised me that he didn't try to console me. Feeling embarrassed and alone, I faced the wall, giving Nat my back, and hugged my bible.

When morning came around, I reluctantly jumped up, grabbed my pink robe, and headed to the bathroom to pray. This was my morning routine. "In Jesus name, I cancel, renounce, and denounce anything that was trying to harm me or come against the plan God has for my life." After my morning prayer, I begin to make breakfast. My plan was to act like the night I had didn't exist. In all actuality, did it really exist or was it a bad nightmare? Nathaniel didn't mention what occurred and neither did I.

Let's rewind a bit to 2018, 2019, and 2020. They were the most difficult years of my whole life. *A Transition From Hell* would be a good title for it. Where do I begin?

In February 2018, while in the JFK airport headed home from a birthday cruise, I received a call from my landlord. I always got nervous when he called because I knew I wasn't current on my rent payments. The birthday trip I had splurged on should have gone towards my rent. However, I was living in a "YOLO" mindset. There was no way to escape the backed up rent I had accumulated. The funds weren't available and the sexual advances from my landlord went unheard. Long story short: I had to go. I learned my lesson and was ready to pay the consequences. That birthday present to myself was very costly. There were many decisions that had to be made.

First, where would I live? My family all had living situations that I didn't want to intrude on. In all honesty, I wasn't that upset about leaving. My only wish was that the horrific issues didn't follow me. The mystery bite marks and bruises would now be a thing of the past. While in my uber, heading home from the airport, I received a random call from Missy. It's funny how God always dispatched angels right when you needed them. Psalms 91:11 declares, "For he will command his angels concerning you." Missy and I started to chat about my trip, which was amazing by the way. That cruise ship didn't know what hit them. My two childhood friends, Keisha and Tiff, really knew how to have fun. We would gather the most amazing footage for Instagram and our own personal memories. People always said we gave them so much life and they lived vicariously through our trips. Oh yes!

Back to the phone conversation. Missy and I chatted about my birthday trip and soon after, the subject shifted to my moving situation. I was embarrassed, so I never disclosed the full details. No one knew the real reason I left my apartment. Pride and ego wouldn't allow me to disclose everything. Even though I knew it wouldn't have mattered, her exact words were, "Sis you know you can always come stay with me right"? That offer was music to my ears. Besides renting a room in someone's house, a NYC shelter may have been my only option. I had heard many foul stories, so

I knew it wouldn't be a walk in the park. After I hung up the phone with Missy, I gave her offer some thought. Even though her house was pretty crowded, I knew I wouldn't be staying long. I was beyond grateful and still I knew, God had placed me there on assignment.

I left my apartment full of memorable items and headed to an unknown territory. My 32-inch flat screen TV, three bins of shoes, and three bags of clothes were all I carried with me. It was bittersweet when I left. I prayed that whatever was tormenting stayed on the premises. The first few days at Missy's house were ok. Most mornings I woke up to Missy's mom screaming. She didn't mean any harm; she was only preparing her grandchildren for the real world. I never witnessed a parent providing so much truth to a six-year-old.

"Listen!! No one is going to give you anything in this damn world. You have to work hard and depend only on yourself."

I could hear her with the door closed. She was ironing Mali's school uniform while giving him a 101 on life. When that alarm clock went off at 6 AM, I rolled my eyes and tapped the sleep icon on my iPhone.

"Good morning sis," I said warmly while climbing over my bestie to get out of the bed we shared. We have been friends since elementary school. I'll never forget the day we met. We clicked instantly. Still to this day we have jokes on drooling Johnny, who we affectionately called Drooly. Elementary school with Missy was a huge comedy show. She called me the ravioli thief. When children would put their lunch trays down to get their chocolate milks, I stole that ravioli like a thief in the night. Sorry God; you snooze, you lose. Those were the days. I stayed with Missy for about a year.

It was so hard to find an affordable apartment; shame on you NYC!! This is why everyone is leaving and going elsewhere. It's hard to maintain a nice apartment alone. Hence why people are shaking up or risking their lives living with roommates they don't know. Within that year, a lot of things were turning around. In that very place, God started to transform me and now it all makes sense. Everything was left behind. I vowed to take the time I was living with Missy to reconstruct my life and bad habits. It seemed like I was in a depressive state. However, I was shedding my old skin. I knew all things were going to work out for my good. Romans 9:28, declares, "And we know that in all things God works for the good of those who love him, who have been called according to his purpose." We must go through the adversities and allow God to order all our steps. Was I A happy camper while everything was taking place? Of course not! It was hard. I took that time to raise my credit, save money, and build an intimate relationship with God.

After 15 years, I decided to go back to college and pursue my degree in counseling. I always dreamed of helping children and teens who battled in some of the same areas that I did. I promised myself I was going to take my education seriously this time around. I still have a plan to create shelters, mentor programs, and pantries for children and adults in need. A coworker at the time, Ms. Nessa had inspired me to get back on track. May God bless Ms. Nessa's soul. She was a victim of the coronavirus during the pandemic of 2020. This pandemic claimed the lives of so many. It showed us how to value everything and not take our loved ones for granted. Ms. Nessa was an angel from God who will truly be missed.

After raising her children, and devoting her life to God, she decided to go back to college. After a couple of decades, she didn't allow the time or new technology to scare her away from her dreams. When I went back to college, I felt a sense of pride. I knew I was taking the necessary steps to change the trajectory of my life. In the past, I was ashamed of not finishing school. I vowed to myself no matter what, I would finish with my Master's Degree. I knew God wanted more for me yet fear always held me back. My days were long. They started at 6 AM and ended around 9 PM. After I finished working with the children, I would head to college until 8 PM and then back home to my friend's couch by 9 PM. Missy and I had gotten a lot closer and we shared so many deep secrets with each other. One thing I noticed about my friends and I, was the pain we shared was a mutual felt pain. We were all pretending to be healed from past wounds, whether it was from our mothers, fathers, ex-boyfriends, or even life itself.

Everyone has a story. I'm glad I was able to spend so much time with Missy and her sons. I think being there filled a void for us both. On some weekends, I worked as a Waiver Service Provider with foster children. My job allowed me to work closely with children and their parents. I took the children on individualized trips to give the parents time to themselves. I considered myself like a big sister. The children really enjoyed having someone to talk to that wouldn't judge them. After our fun times were over, I would come back to their houses and talk to the foster parents about their progression and or any concerns. That job was very eye-opening. It was surprising how a lot of the children were suffering with the bare minimum. Visiting the children at their foster homes touched me. I realized, most of the between children ages of 6-14 lacked a safe haven and were deprived of affection. This hurt me and I always overcompensated with the kids I came in contact with.

While working this job, I knew I was in the right field, and I wanted to make a positive difference. One child I worked with named Marissa was the cutest little thing. She was six years old and had a twin brother named Robert. On Sunday's, Joe, my supervisor and I would go pick up the two children from a huge church on Church Avenue in Brooklyn. It took Marissa a long time to warm up to me. After a few coloring books and Burger King visits, she started smiling more. Eventually, when she saw me waiting for her on Sunday's, she would run to me instead of rolling her eyes. I noticed this was just a defense mechanism.

Marissa didn't want to get too comfortable with me because the people she got comfortable with always left. Her adopted mom barely wanted her around. On Sunday's when Joe and I took that long D train ride towards Coney Island, we sometimes discussed how detached Ms. Bento was towards the children. Ms. Bento was the children's adopted mom. Marissa's biological mom was in jail facing murder charges. We noticed the children were always in their rooms and on separate sides of the house when we came to pick them up from home. When they heard Joe's thick country accent, they would run out of their rooms like captives. We would usually find Ms. Bento sitting on her couch with her biological children in the living room. We would gather the children and then walk past the loud living room that usually played old-school Spanish music. There were many children I worked with and they all held a special place in my heart. I vowed to become a social worker or counselor to help children like Marissa; allowing them to have a personal outlet. It's been about two years and I still think about my little buddies. I had little time to myself as I worked 7 days a week, but I actually liked it that way.

I didn't need much time to sit and ponder. However, I got lonely sometimes. That's pretty much how I met Nick. My routine was getting boring. I figured I should date and live a little. I ended up creating an online profile. Shhhh. Don't tell anyone. I told everyone I met him in Chipotle. Funny story: I catfished Nick because I had a fake profile pic. I figured once I actually liked someone, I would send them my real pictures. There are a lot of deranged people out there and I didn't just want my pictures floating around. Once I viewed Nick's profile, he noticed and contacted me. When I sent him my real pictures after a full conversation, we laughed for about 10 minutes. That joke never got old in our relationship. We clicked from our first conversation. He was very attentive and sweet. We ended up talking about relationships and traveling. Before we knew it, three weeks had passed and we were booking our very first trip to Mexico. We were inseparable. However, there was something I just couldn't understand. Nick was almost perfect. For the first four months, things were ok. It seemed like God had answered my prayers. For the most part, I was happy. We would have cute date nights. We were both foodies, so we were always in the kitchen together. On the weekends and sometimes during the week, his house was my getaway. I enjoyed being there and having peace of mind. He was my safe haven. After a while, the honeymoon stage was over, and everything became a disagreement.

Honestly, I was to blame for a lot of the bickering. I didn't understand why I would become so bothered when he was around. I knew I loved him and was happy to have a breath of fresh air, yet something changed when we came in contact with each other. After we celebrated his birthday, things started to shift. Arguments became intense after I found a lip gloss in his new car, which made me question him all the time. After a heated argument, things got out of hand and Nick broke it off with me after six months. For some reason, I wasn't distraught. I knew everything happened for a reason. I prayed about it and knew God was working it out. I promised God I would be celibate until marriage and I would focus solely on my betterment. Boy, did my life take a twist.

Knuckle Up (War Ready)

For I know the plans I have for you, declares the Lord, plans for welfare and not for evil, to give you a future and a hope. Jeremiah 29:11

After Nick and I broke up, things really started to shift. I was blessed with a new apartment in a beautiful house. There were new appliances and a nice amount of space for me to hook up. Nina had come through for me. I will always have a special place for her in my heart. God sent Nina at the perfect time.

Originally, she was looking for an apartment as well. While viewing the apartment, she felt something in her spirit and knew the place would be right for me. Little did I know, this apartment was going to officially set me free. Nina and I were co-workers who eventually became friends. When I first met her, I thought she was really loud and unpredictable. People like her I usually shied away from. Unexpected dialogue wasn't my type of party. However, Nina became such a staple in my life. She was definitely planted in the midst of my madness. Besides the occasional shadows in my peripheral vision and hearing things drop unexpectedly, my new apartment was bringing me lots of joy. After my breakup, I decided to fast and get closer to God. Nina was also being set free from many adversities. With her knowledge of the spiritual realm, she was helping me a great deal. She would send me tons of YouTube videos and websites to teach me about the Bible and spiritual warfare. I noticed as I studied and became equipped with the word of God, my warfare became more intense. That's how you know you're headed in the right direction when all hell starts breaking loose. You can always tell the size of the blessing by what you have to go through to reach it. By this time, Nick wanted to recant his decision and make things right. I was already too far into my singleness. He tried everything to get me back. He even popped up at my job with beautiful roses. By that time, I had started an intense fast and was focused on the bigger picture. I was praying for clarity and renewal. My mind was tired of going through circles and I needed to be the change I wanted to see. My broken self had no business dating. I was attracting chaos because that's what I was battling inside. Never once did I question God. I always glorified him whether I was hurting or not.

With a very cold tone, I told Nick I wasn't able to get back with him and I wished him the best of luck. It hurt me to know I was hurting his feelings. But I knew this was what I needed to do for me. He shook his head and walked off. That night when I went home, I suffered from two attacks while I tried to sleep. Both times I felt like something was trying to hold me down, not allowing me to move. I got up, prayed, and laid down. From that night on, I slept with my bible on top of my chest. After that encounter, sleeping was a thing of the past. I was scared to be alone, but I had to face my fears. When Sunday came, I made it my business to go to church that morning. I needed some prayer badly. I didn't understand why I was being attacked on such a high level. I sat in my usual spot, but I didn't feel like my usual self. When the choir started to sing, it sounded so angelic that it brought me to tears. Out of nowhere I started screaming and crying uncontrollably. The people at the church barely knew my name. When I came for service, I was quiet and after the service ended, I quietly walked out. That day was different. People looked at me in astonishment. The conservative girl was screaming like someone was killing her and making a scene. My mother knew I was going through a hard time, so she accompanied me to church. When I couldn't stop crying and screaming, a beautiful woman who attended the church walked over to me. She was a member that I spoke to every chance I was able to. I believe she was a deaconess/prophetess. She sat next to me and told me to "Open your eyes." My eyes felt so heavy as if someone was holding them shut. She told me to hold them open if I had too. "They don't want you to look at me." Now, I understand what she meant. I held open my eyes. As she sat in front of me and gazed in, she kept shaking her head compassionately. I could tell God was speaking to her on my behalf. She then grabbed my hand and walked me to the alter to get prayer from the bishop. He laid his hands on my shoulders and prayed for me for about three minutes. When the Bishop was done praying for me, the woman who led me to the altar and my other church friend was waiting to speak to me. She didn't waste any time. "He isn't worth it". Her words hit me like a ton of bricks. There was only one man in my life and I had never mentioned him. I was confused and I didn't want to believe what she was suggesting.

When I got home, I prayed vigorously. I had the privilege of asking Nina for insight because she was battling with a lot of similar situations. It felt good being able to ask her things and not get judged. It was hard holding in all the things that were going on in my life. I was afraid if I told the truth to people they would judge me and think I was insane. By the grace of God, I'm in my right mind. My duty is to be transparent. Only God knows what my readers are battling with right now as they read my testimonies.

May God bless you! Be strong. Your story will be your testimony as well. God gives his hardest battles to his strongest soldiers. Don't carry the load. Surrender.

I started with a 5-day fast and eventually added days. All throughout the bible it explains why fasting is appropriate. If you're looking to get closer to God, fast and pray. There is nothing more intimate than allowing our creator to know that nothing comes before him. He provides the meals and the tables to eat it upon. Why would we not make sacrifices and give up food and worldly items? Fasting is a staple in my life and has changed me for the best. Fasting is basically the act of giving up food, worldly items, and things that you feel like you can't go without. It shows that you don't mind sacrificing for the Lord. I usually withstand food, social media, tv, and anything else that distracts me. Also, while fasting, I indulge in the word of God. I read a bible chapter every couple of hours and most of the time I watched my favorite ministers online. Bishop TD Jakes is my uncle in my head and his daughter Sarah is my cousin. Yes child! They give me so much life.

I often imagined how dope it would be to sit at their tables for dinner as part of their family. I'm sure it would be nothing but laughs and the spread of knowledge. Shout out to Mama Jakes also. You're the real MVP. It takes a special type of woman to oversee so much greatness.

Oh wait! I can't forget my brother from another mother: Michael Todd. I've learned so much from this man. He's so humble. He is exactly what this generation needs. The way he breaks down the bible is brilliant.

Last one, Sophia Ruffin. Drops mic and walks to the kitchen.

Ok, I'm back.

I've caught the Holy Ghost several times watching her YouTube and Facebook videos. What a testimony. So favored. God's grace is amazing, I love her. She taught me how to be my authentic self.

I don't have to hide my sense of humor or be someone I'm not. By the grace of God, I will cast devils out of people wearing my blue, green, or pink hair. Period!! So yes, fasting is definitely a game changer. Remember, it's best to pray and allow God to guide you through your fast. Also do your research because there are many different types of fasting. Don't forget to know the reason why you're fasting and keep a journal of your progress. At that time, I was fasting for clarity, renewal, and to draw closer to God.

Nick was trying to get back in the picture and while I was a little lonely and hurt, I knew I had to be strong. My strength wavered after about two weeks. I prayed and asked God for answers. I felt like God placed it in my heart to take Nick back. However, it was under one circumstance. We had to fast together and he agreed. We fasted for ten days. It made me feel a lot better. At first things were going well, but deep down inside, I felt guilty. I knew things would never be the same. I had tapped into my spirituality. I didn't want to live my same old lifestyle. I viewed people and their actions so much differently. A lot of people thought I was crazy and judgmental, but God was doing a mighty work inside of me. Cheers to an amazing story I will share while on my fast. I was at work getting ready for dismissal in the auditorium. I was standing alone when a couple of my co-workers came to stand next to me. They chatted about how happy they were that it was Friday. I remained quiet while thinking intensely. That day I was wearing a new bracelet that Nick had brought me. I could see my co-worker looking at me from the corner of my eye. A small voice entered my head. "She's going to touch your bracelet." After about three seconds Alice did just that. She walked toward me, reached out her hand, and touched my new bracelet. "That's a nice bracelet," she said with her thick Caribbean accent. I was really in tune with my surroundings. Fasts aren't easy but so necessary to be in tune with God.

I knew Nick was in love with me, but I also knew my new lifestyle was over the top for him. We lived about an hour away from each other. On days when I couldn't sleep, he made his way to come sleep by my side. On the phone, we were great. When we got in person, things changed. We also seemed to bicker. I prayed and asked God for signs to let me know if we weren't for each other. Even though this relationship was very different from all the others, I knew deep down something was missing. I loved Nick and he had such a loving side to him. I admired how he gave his all to the people he loved. He was a little reluctant, but I tried to encourage more prayer within our relationship. I just wanted us to pray before bed, in the morning, and over our dinner.

Sometimes it seemed like I was forcing him, and this created a bit of a strain. Still, we tried to love each other unconditionally. Nick was different than the men I had been involved with. Or maybe this was one of the first times I let someone fight for me. I kept telling myself, just be happy and let things flow naturally. When I started to stay at Missy's house, I prayed for a church home that would allow me to grow spiritually. I enjoyed my bishop's sermons, motivational talks, and generosity, yet, after seven years, I thought I should have grown more in my walk. I honestly felt there was a church that may have been more suitable for my growth. After a few months, I recalled an old conversion myself and my previous supervisor had. He mentioned he and his mom had gone to such an amazing church. He told me that I should try a service one day. Many times that conversation replayed in my mind, so I decided to go to check the church out. It was weird because I felt as if I was cheating on my church that I attended regularly. Yet still, I wanted to visit.

When you can smile and still praise God through the pain, you're unstoppable by his grace and mercy. Speaking of unstoppable! My clothing line Prayer & Hustle was literally birthed in the midst of pain. While I was battling with my faith, torment and flesh, God was working it all out. My friend Tiff, who was a bartender, started making and selling her own drinks independently. During the summer, she went to events and sold her beverages. There was a popular event going on in Brooklyn that everyone knew about. It was in Brownsville, Brooklyn and the event was called Old Timers Day. This was a 2 Day event and one that people from all over Brooklyn were very fond of. Locals came out to see familiar faces, listen to oldies but goodies, and buy tasty soul food. At this event, you would be able to catch people doing the electric slide and twerking all in the same space. There was so much harmony in the atmosphere. We stayed for a few hours having fun with no incidents; just love. Even though Brownsville didn't have the best reputation, people could honestly say they felt safe that night.

However, later after we left, we received news that twelve people were shot and one killed. R.I.P to the man who lost his life. Before we left, we laughed, joked, and ate some bomb soul food. I still remember that fish sandwich to this day. We also came up with an idea to host a pop-up shop to make some extra money. Keisha was playing with the thought of starting a seafood catering business and Tiff had the beverages. I knew I wanted to be on board so I thought about doing something that would magnify God and bring extra funds.

Eventually, I started a motivational clothing line. Prayer & Hustle embodies everything we need to survive. First prayer, then the determination to move forward, and use your God given talents to make an impact (hustle). We also included another mutual friend Mandy who sold beautiful mink lashes. We put our thinking caps on and came up with such a dope event. We were blown away with all the support we received.

Throughout the planning process, I noticed the growth in all of us. God was taking us all in different directions. We all chose to embrace that movement. It felt really good to be a business owner as I always had a love for fashion and designing clothes. My advice to you is do something you love when starting a business and it won't seem like work. No matter what you're doing, always make sure God approves of this business. Everything we do, we must take it up in prayer. Our father wants the very best for us. He won't lead us wrong.

True story: for two weeks I struggled to come up with a logo design. Nick was so over me, but I was determined to come up with my logo. When I'm working on a project, I'm fixated. After stressing myself out, I took a prayer and meditation break. After a few minutes, I started to imagine designs in my head. I began to scribble in my book. Before I knew it, my logo design was complete. I was amazed. Prayer works and God is awesome!

Finding My Way Back

For where two or three are gathered in my name, there am I among them. "
Matthew 18:20 ESV

There is something about walking in a new church for the first time that makes you so jittery. You're basically going into the unknown, almost like visiting a friend and walking through the living room full of their family watching tv. Embarrassment had completely pushed me out of my church and I was afraid to go back and be remembered as the screaming girl. So, I prayed and was led to a church that felt more like home. I couldn't shake it. It's like God was telling me to go there. After I was done getting dressed, I would normally put on a shade of lipstick to match my clothes. As I reached into my makeup bag for my fuchsia pink lipstick, there was an unexpected urge for me not to wear it. That day, I also wore the bare minimum because usually I stood out with unique clothing pieces. That Sunday I wanted to fit in, not stand out. As I told you guys, I am a lover of fashion. Sometimes without acknowledging it, I would over dress. God didn't want people to notice my clothes, shoes, or my hair at first. He wanted me to be humble. After I got off the C train and started my journey to my new church, I felt something in my spirit saying today you will join this church.

When I reached the end of the block, I came across such a beautiful church building. I'm sure the congregation was delighted in calling this church home. I walked up the stairs to the main entrance where I encountered the friendliest woman. I immediately took a liking to her. After a few moments, I was handed a program and ushered to my seat. When we reached an empty row, I was greeted by a middle-aged man who was very sweet. His name was Gary. He shook my hand firmly and introduced himself very warmly. In the middle of our chatting, the choir began to sing. Initially, I couldn't get into the music. The young man who played the organ was out of tune. My mind started to wander. The enemy then began to creep in my mind. I asked myself, "Am I in the right place?" God knows I love music. Then, I heard such an amazing voice that regulated the small mishaps of the organ player. I regained my focus because her voice was so unique. I believe she was an alto. The therapeutic, soulful melodies that came from her were ministering to me. I've noticed during my journey that God anoints people's gifts. You don't have to be the best singer, dancer, or minister. However, he will use you to get to his children.

God will bless you abundantly when you use your gifts and talents to magnify him. Shortly after the song selection, the pastor stood to speak. He was such a modest yet confident man. He didn't raise his voice or perspire. Yet his sermons were effective and his messages penetrated. After about an hour and a half, he opened the doors of the church. This action allowed new people to join. A flashback then came to my mind. I remembered the message I received walking to the church a couple of hours ago. My legs felt as though bricks were on top of them. I wasn't able to stand or move. I became really nervous. The pastor announced again, "Will there be one who is coming forth today? "The doors of the church are still open." I leaped out of my seat as if I had just broken free. I began to power walk down the church aisle. It seemed like the longest walk ever. With tears streaming from my face, I knew this was the beginning of a new me. I felt relieved. Each step I took, I could feel chains breaking off my life. The congregation started to clap for me, and I figured they all knew about the trauma and demonic activity I had been through. At that moment, my old church flashed before my eyes. I would miss the people there, but God was doing something special. The fight was over. I was submitting to the plan my father had for me. The Lord knew growth would take place there. After a couple of months, I became familiar with my new church family. Everyone was friendly and I loved how they celebrated our pastor and his great works. There was a lot of unity. After a few months, I thought it would be a great idea to get re-baptized for my new beginning. After taking new membership classes, I was finally eligible for my re-baptism.

On my special day, while preparing myself to get dressed, I noticed the familiar face of a beautiful brown skin older woman.

"Here you go baby, change into this," ' she said in the sweetest voice as she passed me my white attire. I needed to wear all white during the baptism.

"Hello," I said. "You look very familiar," I said to the woman with bold beautiful features.

"Really?" she said.

"I was with the Board of Education for many years; you may have been one of my students."

Long story short, she turned out to be my cousin.

"Her better half," which she affectionately called her longtime partner did the honor of baptizing me. Look at God. He was showing me that he was preparing a table that only he put together. Listen to that small voice my people. God doesn't misguide his children.

While my spiritual life was flourishing, everything else was hanging on by strings. I tried my best to stay positive and happy. However, I felt my happiest when I was in church, listening to gospel music, or viewing Christian sermons. Nick and I were still together, going on getaways, and planning cute dates. There was something missing though. I felt guilty for forcing him into my new lifestyle. I had 110% dedicated my life to God and I knew it wouldn't be an easy transition for him because it wasn't his choice. Hence why I was always trying to smoothly break things off with him. He held on with all his might. He wouldn't let me go, no matter how much we went through. I told him it was fine if he had a change of mind. His favorite line was "I'll adjust." When he got really upset, he would tell me he knew that he was in our relationship to prepare me for someone else. Now, that statement makes so much sense.

Eventually, I started to miss my old lifestyle and little by little, I would slip back in old worldly ways. It was pleasurable for the moment. However, I started to feel uncomfortable with drinking, smoking, and fornicating. God was condemning me. I knew I wouldn't be able to play both sides of the fence for much longer and still keep my promises to myself and God. On top of all the things I was going though, my sleeping patterns were still off. Really strange things would take place in my apartment even when Nick was there. Sometimes we would wake up from having the same dreams. After being introduced to the seriousness of dreams, I started to do lots of research. Many people don't know but your dreams are indications and most times warning signs of the occurrences that are taking place in the spiritual realm. Yes, it's very deep. Don't ignore your dreams, guys.

Throughout the bible, God speaks to people through their dreams. "In the last days, God says, I will pour out my Spirit on all people. Your sons and daughters will prophesy, your young men will see visions, your old men will dream dreams," according to Acts 2:17. Let's be clear, the enemy also shows up in your dreams. When he comes, he always brings havoc upon you. I watched several videos on YouTube from different ministers. By the grace of God, my eyes were opened to many things. The enemy can't attack you while you're awake, therefore, in dreams, he goes after his victims, prowling like a hungry lion.

Ever dream you're eating, seeing dirty shoes, or having sexual intercourse while dreaming? Yup, these are all ploys from the enemy. I was bombarded at one point in time with dreams from the enemy. I noticed there was a connection to the dreams I was having and sickness. My second home was urgent care for medical services. I was having impure thoughts and many sicknesses that seemed to overtake me. My immune system was terrible, especially when I would wake up from bad dreams. I felt sick.

Prayer and vigorous fasting helped me so much. After speaking to Nina, she sent me many scriptures to decree and declare over my life. She had also sent me a prayer that I recited every time I woke up from a nap or full night of sleep. To give a synopsis of the prayer, it was basically canceling any dreams, plans, or deterrence from the enemy or anyone that was from the kingdom of darkness. It was a long prayer; however, I included it in my daily schedule every day. It was as important to me as me showering and brushing my teeth. Thank you, Lord, for changing my life!

Sometimes, I get so full of joy thinking about God's grace. I beg of you if you don't have a relationship with Jesus Christ our Lord and Savior, please get one! It will change your life for the better. Once you start making time and professing your love, he will work wonders in your life. I dare you to give him a chance.

On our 1-year anniversary, Nick gave me such an amazing promise ring. I was a little confused about the title of the ring but after a few heated discussions, I understood where he was coming from. Our relationship had been complicated from the very beginning. Yet we both made an effort to get through it together. The ring was a gesture that he was with me for longevity. "When I finally pop the question, your ring will be even better than that one." I was all smiles because the ring he had brought was already a mouth dropper. I was excited to see what the next ring would look like. It was awkward wearing such an extravagant ring though. So many people congratulated me after they saw it. Yet, I was lost for words on how to reply. It wasn't an engagement ring. After one year, my 33-year-old self was getting a promise ring. I didn't want to sound ungrateful, yet I still needed to be honest. I wanted people to just stop asking me. At one point Nick and I laid in the bed and slept together without having sex for four months before I gave in. Some people thought he was crazy, but I knew it was love. I was battling myself at this point, with confusion and doubt. It was bad.

The first Saturday of every month, ten other women including myself gathered to magnify the Lord at Nina's house. We laughed, cried, worshiped, and worshipped some more. It felt good to be transparent with each other. We were all battling with obstacles. However, we had each other's backs. All of us had bright futures. There, I formed some unwavering friendships. Better yet: sisterhoods. When Godly women come together, supernatural things start to take place. Chains break, families are restored, and Godly kingdoms are enhanced! After sharing my issues with sleeping, Shaunna gave me some great advice.

"Sis, put bible verses all over your house, play bible scriptures while sleeping and praise the lord like you lost your mind. The enemy is going to think something is wrong with you."

I'll never forget that. Ha-ha. I did exactly what she said and after a while, things were getting better. I was happier and getting closer to our creator. The meetings always left us feeling empowered by each other. The Holy Spirit was in attendance every time we were together. The sleeping issues I had suffered with for half my life were becoming a thing of the past! Yes!! **(Plandemic 2020)**

"Never Would Have Made It"

I have said these things to you, that in me you may have peace. In the world you will have tribulation. But take heart; I have overcome the world." John

16:33

C oronavirus 2020 was in full effect and holding no punches. God was having his way. He wanted everyone to be still and wait on him for mercy. What we chose to do in this detrimental waiting period marked the outcome of our future. I chose to plan! I chose to get closer to God and obey him in all aspects of my life. I was literally led by the Holy Spirit in everything I did. The pandemic had struck in other countries, yet, the United States was hit the hardest. We had a record-breaking number of deaths. As a proud New Yorker, I can attest to us being the city that never sleeps. The pandemic stripped us of everything we were. I knew something amazing was about to happen because of the adversities that were taking place. After the pandemic started, it was a downward spiral. My co-workers and I were very nervous. We were employees of the Department of Education and we worked very closely with children. Schools were a common place for people to carry germs and viruses. After a few long weeks of deliberating, the government officials finally closed schools. Soon after, everyone was stuck in the house besides essential workers. The unemployment rate reached 2.5 million in the month of May 2020. The last day my church gathered before the lock down was my pastor's anniversary. It was such a pivotal celebration that I was happy to be a part of. The love was felt all throughout the building. Following the service, food and dessert was served. My instincts were telling me to go home. Yet, the way my stomach was set up I did the opposite. I stood in a hefty line for fried fish and all the trimmings; mac and cheese, collard greens, and yams to name a few. For dessert, they served the tastiest white chocolate strawberries. My tummy was very happy. I took the best seat in the house. I had the pleasure of sitting next to the funniest man in the church. We talked about how good the food was and afterwards, we cracked some jokes. Only if I could remember his name.

When I arrived home, I noticed that my skin was really warm. At that moment, I was wishing I had ordered that thermometer from Amazon. I took a shower and headed straight to bed when I started feeling fatigue. My mind started racing. "You better not have coronavirus", I said to myself about ten times. Why didn't I just go home? I thought long and hard until I drifted off to sleep.

When I woke up the next morning, I had the same headache I fell asleep with. The heaviness in my body wouldn't allow me to move off the bed. At that very moment, I knew I had to take control.

The enemy was not going to catch God's child slipping. Nope. I said a prayer then proceeded to plead the blood of Jesus all over my body. "I plead your blood all over my body Jesus, please heal me." I spoke boldly and I wanted the enemy to know he was not in control, but he was under my feet. I kept confessing Psalms 91 over my life. Then I followed up by pleading the blood of Jesus over every inch of my temple.

"Jesus, I plead the blood over my head. I plead the blood over my brain. I plead the blood over my arms and legs. Thank you in advance for your healing, dear Lord. I am healed by the mighty stripes of the Jesus!" I shouted.

Then, I moved in faith off the bed. Ladies and gentlemen, spoiler alert. You're already healed and no weapon formed against you will ever prosper. Let no sickness or doctor report bind you up! We have a healer who walks with us daily. End of story. Let's leave our faith in our creator's hand. Thank you, Jesus, for the ultimate sacrifice you made. We worship you!

I jumped out of bed and dropped to my knees in a thankful cheer. That was one of many coronavirus scares. As you can see, the Lord won every time. Nick and I were both getting sick back-to-back. I thought it would be a good idea if we kept our distance and both nurtured ourselves in solitude. He was an essential worker, so he was constantly around homeless people and the public.

Dear Essential Workers,

You guys are the real MVP's! So many noble people lost their lives while serving the public.

Thank You,

Toneika

Most workers were trying their best to earn an honest paycheck to feed their families. Let's have a moment of silence for all the essential workers who lost their lives serving the community. May God continue to bless all of their souls.

God was revealing so many things during the pandemic to me. He showed me that solitude would be my best friend and worst enemy. What will I say? I wasn't the same after it ended. My faith began to increase in the Lord. I was home alone, scared, confused, and oblivious to what would happen next. My mother called me the *boy in the bubble*. I was afraid to let anyone come into my house, including her. I also limited going outside to once every three weeks. That was only for food and shopping purposes. I was living in isolation. At times it was frustrating, lonely, and tedious, however I knew God had something up his sleeve. After a month of being in the unknown, I held on to faith as if it was going out of style. Something was shifting in me. I wasn't the same. My thoughts and my vision for my life had changed. What I needed could only be received by submitting and giving my life to the Lord. That meant no more premarital sex, no more drinking to get drunk, or acting a fool. When I tell you I was the life of the party when I went out, I meant it! Don't get me wrong, I still can cut a rug. For the youngings, that means to command the dance floor and work up a sweat.

Jesus didn't die so I could continue acting a fool. He died so my sins would be forgiven. He died so I could live the life that is best for myself and his kingdom. Will God still love you if you drink, smoke, and twerk? Of course. What father turns his back on his children when they have made mistakes? Still make it right and live a life that you and God can be proud of.

I don't have many stories about my father. I'll use my grandmother, Clatis, instead. Growing up, I had some rebellious ways. I was always going against the things my grandmother said. As I grew older, I realized my rebelliousness stemmed from the lack of proper attention from my parents. My grandma was an amazing role model and provider. She was overprotective but now I'm thankful for that.

Clatis Williams was my CO, PO, and security guard. I was her precious jewel, and she didn't play about me. On the weekends I would sneak off the block where I was supposed to stay. Some days I didn't come back for hours, leaving my grandmother in the window for long periods of time. I would forget my grandmother was in the window watching me until I heard a squeaky voice calling my name. "Tonekiaaaaaa!," she would yell, stretching out every syllable in my name. I'm sure everyone on the block knew my government. I hated it back then but now I know it was all out of love. No matter what I did or what type of grief I gave my grandmother, she always received me, waiting at the window for her baby to return. That's the same love that God has for us but even greater.

Most of my life I lived by satisfying my flesh and needs. During my transitional time, I wanted to sacrifice the rest of my years serving the almighty, living in peace, and enjoying a clean lifestyle. Consequently, Nick didn't agree. I was torn about my decisions, yet, I knew it had to be done. God honors clean hearts and ways for his kingdom. Giving up my relationship was a huge sacrifice for me. I knew I couldn't live out my calling going against God's word. I wanted a clean slate, so Nick and I decided to go our separate ways.

I worried about him often. He had a hard life as a child. Something we had in common was pain and trauma. Deep down I wanted to protect him. There was a little boy inside of him who had never healed. He acted as if he was superman, however I knew at times he wanted to run and hide from this cold world. I still keep him in my prayers. People thought I was crazy when I told them we had broken up. I grew tired of explaining why, so I just stopped. My advice will always be to follow God. He knows better than we do.

During the pandemic, I learned so much about myself. My daily life consisted of solitude, prayer, fasting, contemplating, planning, and more solitude. Being alone for a long time can only do two things. It can bring you to the verge of mental insanity or allow you to focus on God for strength and sanity. Thank you, Father, for my strength and sanity. Did I ever question how things would transpire? Yes. Did I know God was rebuilding me for a wonderful testimony? Absolutely. Still, things got worse before they got better.

Gratefully Broken

Crazy Faith

He said to them, "Because of your little faith. For truly, I say to you, if you have faith like a grain of mustard seed, you will say to this mountain, 'Move from here to there,' and it will move, and nothing will be impossible for you."

Matthew 17:20

Wow, where do I start?

Sis, you are about to be on fire for the Lord." Her words dropped on me like another Funk Master Flex bomb. Shanna had prophesied to me during a ministry zoom call. She kept saying, "Wow. Wow sis. People are not even going to know who you are. Watch what the Lord is about to do in your life."

During my transition, I noticed only the strong survive. You have to submit to God and listen to the still small voice. How can we hear that voice if our minds are cluttered? How can we hear that voice if the people around us are occupying our attention? How can we hear that voice if all our time is spent on social media or gossiping? We will never hear God's voice if we don't sacrifice time and worldly escapes.

According to Psalms 32:8:9, "God will instruct us and teach us all the ways we should go." Have patience and most importantly have faith. After about two weeks, another anointed woman had released a word from God. After that weekly meeting I received a message from Nina. She had forwarded a message someone sent her privately. I had never met this beautiful soul before our prayer meeting. However, God delivered another word through another one of his precious vessels. The message read; "God calls Tonekia humble and holy. He is saying he hasn't forgotten her. He calls her an administrator." I received that word. God had me feeling like I could walk on water. I was so delighted with what God was doing for me in that season. He will take you through the fire, in order to prepare for the places that he has only prepared for you. He'll never let go of your hand.

The pandemic taught me not to take anything for granted. We went a few months living in the unknown. Still, I knew the same God that held my hand all my life was walking by my side now. Since people couldn't attend their church institutions, we had to follow our church leaders online via Facebook, Instagram, and YouTube. This was actually a blessing. It allowed me and many other people I knew to rebuild our faith and relationships with God. We wanted to know the Lord for ourselves and beg for his strength that was created in our weakness. During this pandemic I should've created a business plan for knee pads or a cushioned rug because I stayed on my knees most of the day praying. Maybe that's not a bad idea. Y'all better not try to steal my idea. Haha.

My spiritual sister Shanna introduced me to such an anointed man, who later became my spiritual father: Apostle Omar Morton. My first time watching his sermon I knew it was something so peculiar about him and his teachings. He was full of wisdom and confidence. I stayed up a few nights until 4 AM praying with the congregation, who was extremely hungry for the Lord. This man was so diligent. Every night from 2 AM to 4 AM he would pray on Facebook. I begin to notice supernatural things happening. I was very in tune and something was connecting inside of me. The feeling was very familiar. After about two weeks of sermons, teachings, and prayer, I couldn't get enough. The spiritual food I was receiving was fulfilling to my soul. I was also having many visions while I was in constant prayer. God was revealing so many things to me: specific details about my present and future. My Savior was giving me answers to so many unanswered issues in my life. The same people who tried to redirect me in life, were soon going to see the grace and mercy of the Lord.

Soon after, Apostle O encouraged his congregation to join him on a fast. The purpose of the fast was for healing, our government system, and to bring the body of Christ in unity with our creator. I had no idea this fast would change my life. The fast started out pretty intense. I agreed to give up Instagram, which had a stronghold on me. I also wouldn't eat from 12 AM to 5 PM the next day. For someone who loved food as much as me, this was hard. All day I dreamed of jerk chicken and fried fish sandwiches with hot sauce and ketchup. Yet, I knew me getting closer to God was more important than food or social media.

While praying one night, I received the strangest yet most vivid vision. The vision started by me being attacked by what looked like the grim reaper. This demon spirit had a long white face and wore a hooded long black gown. In the vision, the odd looking spirit being kept trying to come close to me and attack me. Then an image of Jesus came to my rescue. Jesus was literally fighting off the demonic figure for me. Jesus started sweeping the figure out a nearby door. That scream looking figure (the movie scream) would not leave me alone. He kept bussing through doors to find me. Then Jesus proceeded to get gangsta. He slapped the hooded figure who happened to be very persistent. After that wake-up call, the enemy knew that Jesus wasn't playing about me. Jesus was willing to fight over and over for me. Take that! Take that! (In my Diddy voice)

Psalm 46:1 emphasizes that "God is our refuge and strength, very present help in trouble." When I tell you our Savior is good, that's an understatement. God was showing me that he was literally fighting my battles. He also showed me what I needed to continue to pray against. He knew there were demonic beings in the natural and supernatural world who were against me. I chose to give up everything in exchange for a righteous life. God was giving me insight to what was trying to hold me back. Many people don't understand the power of the Lord. He will get down in the dirt with you. I am a living testimony of forgiveness and grace. God has many plans for me and these plans were created while I was in my mother's belly. After my vision that seemed like a 3D dream, I opened my eyes and started praising the Lord like my life depended on it. So many supernatural things started to take place during this earth shaking fast. Later that day I rushed on Facebook to check out the teachings that Apostle O was about to go into. He was always so informative and gave you the truth and nothing but the truth. He is a hardworking man who genuinely cares about his congregation's well-being. He taught us how to fight with the fire of prayer. The jewels he gives us are critical in our walk with the Almighty. He has ministered that in order to be fruitful, we must pray hard, sacrifice, and be diligent in God's word.

Apostle O is also a Brooklynite. He came up from the tough streets of Forte Green, Brooklyn. God took him through a road of destruction to rebuild him for His glory only. The powerful 2 AM prayers changed my life. I'll never forget when the Apostle Omar Morton gave me a word from the Lord. He had no knowledge he was giving me confirmation, but he was speaking in the spirit and the word he spoke was for me. "God is telling me, "He is slapping the enemy for you." Those words came out slowly and went straight inside my ear gages. God was slapping the demonic figure in my vision. Now God was confirming what he did.

"Lord," I said while I looked in the sky, "thank you."

At that very moment, I knew it wouldn't be easy but I was walking on faith and pursuing the calling on my life to be the woman on fire that God wanted me to be.

When I sacrificed and started living in my purpose, my life became so more meaningful. No longer was I holding on to people or situations that were pulling me back. The weight was gone.

Now I sleep better, my prayer life has been strengthened, and I'm knocking these goals out 1 by 1. I refuse to let my past dictate who I will become. Every day I declare I am wealthy, healthy, and victorious! There is nothing you can't do when you pray and have an intimate relationship with our creator. Out do the old you! Let go of the old.

Turn Down For What!

Final Thoughts

Wow, where do I start?

So I "Unmuted Myself" in 2020 with my first book. It was co-authored with some women that I now call my sisters. Nine months later, my water broke with another book baby. During that process I went from "Hurting to Healing" with my second co-authored book. This journey was one of a kind. I was able to go forth with some of my sisters whom I labored in prayer with during the pandemic. Two words: life-changing!

Now, baby, look who is on her 3rd book and first solo project!!

Do you good people see what God has done?

I was Gratefully broken!! Do you know what that means? My whole life I felt less than, but this is only the beginning.

My life has been filled with trials, errors, and let downs. However, what people saw as a mess, God saw as a message. My life is a message to other people. I've lost loved ones who meant the world to me. I've lost jobs, apartments, and men who I thought would love me forever!

But sis didn't lose her faith!! Okurrrrr.

I'm still living! I'm still striving. No one can break what God has made. No matter what you've been through, victory is already yours. You've been knocked down a couple of times but so what!! You will not give up because giving up is not in your DNA. Jesus never gave up. He carried that cross so we can live our best lives. Forgive the people who talked about you, forgive your parents, and most importantly forgive yourself. There are people who are waiting for your beautiful, healed self. Walk tall so your crown WON'T fall.

Don't give up on your dreams.

You will be successful in everything you do.

Stop doubting yourself.

Pain is not your color; shame is not your fragrance.

What you did last year is not your business anymore.

God gives us new mercy every day.

God turned my whole life into a testimony.

I went from twerking in the club to waking up every night for 2AM prayer calls.

I refuse to be anything less than an inspiring author, multi-business owner, and a true woman of God.

Wear your battle wounds with pride.

They made you exactly who you are.

That's why you can't be duplicated.

Repeat after me:

I was Gratefully Broken; that's my superpower!

Meet The Author

Tonekia Williams is a Brooklyn, New York native, who lives by the Bible Scripture in Philippians 4:13 that states, "I can do all things through Christ who strengthens me".

For most of Tonekia's career, she has served others in the capacity of either being an Educator, Clothing Designer, Human Service Representative, or Philanthropist. Tonekia believes her contribution to the world is larger than her existence. She is eager to share her God given talents to help others by any means. As a new author, she vows to tell her whole truth in order to help people overcome their hidden pain.